What
are
you
doing
with
the
rest
of
your
life?

What are you doing with the rest of your life?

CHOICES IN MIDLIFE

PAULA PAYNE HARDIN

NEW WORLD LIBRARY

SAN RAFAEL CALIFORNIA

© 1992 Paula Payne Hardin, Ed.D.

Published by New World Library
58 Paul Drive
San Rafael, CA 94903

Cover design: Kathy Warinner
Text design & Typography: TBH/Typecast
Word Processing: Deborah Eaglebarger
Back cover photograph: Marcia Heeter

Library of Congress Cataloging-in-Publication Data

Hardin, Paula Payne, 1933-
  What are you doing with the rest of your life? : choices in midlife / Paula Payne Hardin.
    p. cm.
  ISBN 0-931432-89-8 (acid-free paper)
    1. Middle age—United States. 2. Middle aged persons—United States – Psychology. I. Title.
  HQ1059.5.U5H37 1992
  305.24'4 – dc20   91-42334
                     CIP

ISBN 0-931432-89-8
Printed in the U.S.A. on acid-free paper
10 9 8 7 6 5 4 3

To Erik H. Erickson—
who provided us with a framework
for thinking about our lives,
and whose response to my work
felt like a benediction.
Thank you.

Contents

Acknowledgments

NONE OF US IS ALONE, and none of us accomplishes anything alone. It follows that this book is the result of the efforts of many influences, known and unknown. The process, beginning with my study of adult development to seeing this book as an expression of my work, has taken ten years. I acknowledge all my teachers – my family, friends, enemies, institutions, nature, and the Wisdom that is all around us.

Certain names especially come to mind: Sharan Merriam for helping me learn to think more clearly; Madeleine L'Engle for opening up my writing style; Sue Baugh for calling forth my courage by taking my roughest of beginner's drafts and making sense of them with her editing skills. I am so grateful to Geralyn Vankerschaever and Steven Lindquist for keeping my body working and helping me sort out my life.

My core community has opened me to the wonder and power of love as we learned to be real with one another. Thank you David, Titia and Bill Ellis, Marianne and Bill Johnson.

One of the most valuable contributions to my life and to this book is from Jan Stein, who midwifed the birth of my true Self with skill and love unmeasurable.

Without the gift of Marilyn McGuire, my agent, who saw potential in my work, I couldn't have found Carol LaRusso at New World Library. Carol had the faith that this work could be turned into something useful for others and has guided me line by line.

But the biggest of hugs goes to my husband, David, who encouraged, prodded, did dishes, and read my work many, many times. He is a one-person cheering section!

Introduction

THE PHONE RANG. My friend Nancy had just returned from a visit with her eighty-year-old mother on the East Coast.

"Paula, I thought about your research and teaching work so often while visiting my mother. I found myself just collapsing, regressing into a childish role around her. She's so negative and self-centered. I'd ask her how she slept; she'd say, 'Awful.' I'd ask her how she felt and she'd say, 'Terrible.' I'd encourage her to come to Illinois and visit more often and she'd say, 'I can't do that, who'll drive me to the airport?' as though it was impossible to take a taxi.

"Paula, Mother will never change. She'll stay in that big house, feel sorry for herself, and try to make the rest of us feel guilty. She's absolutely miserable—and it's just getting worse. Toward the end of the trip I found myself clenching my jaws all the time—I talked to Mother through clenched jaws!"

Nancy is a woman with a reputation for taking things in stride, yet what she was confronting overwhelmed her. Nancy was witnessing the painful process of her mother becoming a burden to herself, to her family, and to society. She was afraid for her mother's future and its impact on her own life. Anna, Nancy's mother, is an example of unsuccessful aging.

Facing Life's Challenging Journey

We come into the world full of potential that can be encouraged or repressed. Each of us is dealt a unique set of circumstances, liabilities, and resources, and it is our responsibility to sort these out and nurture our lives. We must learn to play the hand that has been dealt to us with skill, integrity, and imagination, so that our promise is nurtured and not lost.

Each of us sculpts our destiny every day of our lives, and at the same time, we are sculpted upon. Inner and outer forces and events shape and reshape us continuously. Each new stage in life presents us with different challenges, and it takes courage and flexibility to live through these passages fully and vitally.

Most of us face hazards in the course of our lives, especially after age forty or so, which may include sickness, loss, financial reversals, divorce, or loneliness. We may suffer from broken dreams, forced retirement, or reduced circumstances. Loved ones can be ungrateful and thoughtless. Tragedies, physical deterioration, deaths of friends or family—all these can visit us.

Some people fail to negotiate adversity well; they fall into chronic anger, joylessness, unnecessary physical deterioration, or isolation. Sometimes despair, low vitality, complaints, and even meanness of spirit rule their daily lives. Others, however, seem to have found something valuable, enduring, and joyous in life in spite of obvious difficulties. This group has made contact with a creative inner core, and has gained strength, humor, wisdom, and much more.

What is this inner core? This is only one way of describing an essential aspect of ourselves—some call it the inner self, the higher self, the real self, the center, or the God within. Whatever the name, it feels like "home" when we connect with it. Swiss psychiatrist and innovative thinker, Carl Jung, used the simple word Self with a capital "S" to indicate that this essential place in us is connected to that which is greater than our individual identity. This concept of inner core is a key theme throughout the book.

Those who have connected with their inner core can face life's inevitable hazards with nourishing resources. Their sense of meaning and their belief in themselves has grown until it has become unshakable. Richly connected to others and to something greater than themselves, their lives have a compelling personal grace and naturalness. But some, like Nancy's mother, don't fare so well in the later years of life.

What went wrong in Anna's life? This basically well-intentioned, religiously inclined woman slipped onto a negative track—and stayed there. It is easy to do. Some inevitable disappointments and losses came to her and she fell under the load. In her pain she began to blame others for not rescuing her. She began to see people only in terms of how they could meet her needs. As Anna spent her energies trying to make others fit into her life scheme and play the parts she wanted them to play, she alienated the ones she truly needed. Trying to control others and force them to change to fulfill our expectations will not work. Anna's desperate attempts sabotaged her ability to shape her life and engage in the task of exercising the only true power any of us really has—the power to change ourselves.

Aging well does not mean the absence of problems. It does mean we can choose to prepare for and recognize a fork in the road that comes to us during the second half of life. We can recognize some problems that may confront us as we grow older. We can learn to avoid unnecessary suffering, and focus on attitudes and activities that bring us joy and fulfillment.

This book is about looking with courage and honesty at the road on which you are traveling during your life journey—noticing in what direction you are going, and checking to see if this is the way you really want to go. I hope you bend your ear toward the deep inner call that comes to you in midlife, urging you to become more than you realize you are.

I have looked at the phenomenon of the middle years as a gateway to the second half of life through the eyes and experiences of many people, and have listened from various levels and perspectives. My method has been to walk around this subject and catch a few of its many facets. I've painted word pictures of my observations and experiences rather than moving linearly from one point to the next.

Although the inequities and wrongs in our social systems and institutions often discourage our human promise, I believe that creative social change comes from the grassroots—from you and me. So I have focused in this book on how we can claim the power of our middle years and together become a force for good.

Kahlil Gibran observed, "The river continues on its way to the sea, broken the wheel of the mill or not." Time keeps moving us, like a river, inexorably along to our destination whether we are productively engaged with life's flow or not. We can learn to tap into the life-flow, the Tao, and when we do, life gains the effortless beauty of which the wise ones speak.

We can learn to form a partnership with time, harnessing the energy of the river of life. We can engage the mill wheel with creativity and skill so it grinds the flour to make the bread that nourishes us and those around us. And when we do, we will find we are supported, guided, and blessed beyond what we could imagine—we will find Life a generous giver.

PART I

The challenges

CHAPTER ONE

Successful, Unsuccessful Aging

Don't aim at success—the more you aim at it and make it a target, the more you are going to miss it. For success, like happiness, cannot be pursued; it must ensue . . . as the unintended side-effect of one's personal dedication to a course greater than oneself.

—VICTOR FRANKL

I FEEL MY LIFE, like a river, moving steadily through the years and I am powerless to stop this process called aging. Questions plague me now in a way I have never experienced before and I feel restless, afraid.

There are plenty of people around me who are models for various ways of getting older. I look at some of their lives and know I want mine to be different. I wonder what part of the aging process I can influence. I want to find out and learn from those who are further along in life and who are richly aging.

In the night when I cannot still my mind, something keeps asking: "What's ahead for you?" "How can you live so that your future is fun, rewarding, and useful?" "Will you

3

have decent health, enough money?" "What do you *really* want to do, have, give, and be in the years ahead?" "What do you need to accomplish so you feel your life has counted for something good?"

When I turned fifty I finally let myself realize just how afraid I was. Some people do it sooner—maybe I am a late bloomer. I didn't expect depression because my fortieth birthday had sailed by and I had congratulated myself on looking and feeling young. Turning fifty was different. It was a real marker event for me. The term "half-a-century" kept roving through my mind.

For three days I could hardly get out of bed. I knew that I had to stop denying a lot of things, stop playing the game of fooling myself. Time was inexorably moving me on and I felt helpless before its power. Fears I had not faced before reared their heads, forcing themselves into my thoughts. I felt compelled to look on the unthinkable: what if I turned into a miserable old person, lonely, sick, a burden to myself and others? It was one of my possible futures.

More of Us Are Living Longer

Over the past few decades, there has been a dramatic increase in the average human life expectancy in the United States. For example, those born in 1900 expected to live about forty-seven years. That was the average. Today's average life expectancy is about seventy-six. Twenty-nine extra years have been added to life for most of us, some-times even more. What an opportunity—what a challenge!

This extension of life is seen by some as a problem, a burden on society. Programs designed to assist people in their later years are faltering under the weight of sheer numbers: Social Security is in trouble; Medicare is fraught

4

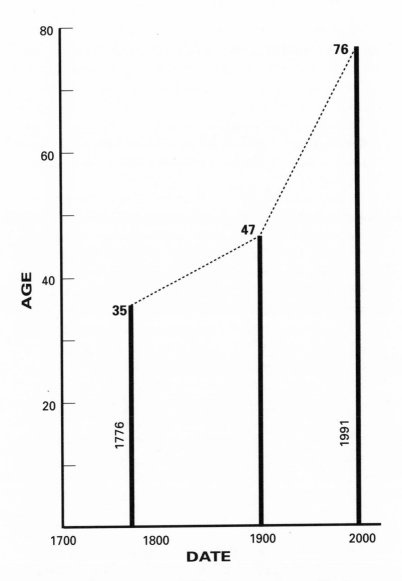

U.S. Average Life Expectancy Rate

Adapted from U.S. census data

with inequities. Many families feel burdened by the increasing demands of frail, elderly parents. Our society appears unprepared for the twenty-first-century challenge of a greatly extended lifetime, and we have many questions and concerns.

Fears of aging haunt us. What does it mean to be old? What does it feel like? When is one old? How do you tell? What is it like to be in middle life, no longer young but certainly not yet old?

How do we care for greater numbers of old people without over-burdening the young? Is life-support at any price a realistic and culturally useful goal? Are some of our medical breakthroughs sabotaging our right to die with dignity?

One visit to a nursing home and we are sobered: palsied hands, blank eyes, wheelchairs, missing teeth, diapers, unpleasant smells, childishness, loss of dignity, suffering, irrelevancy, boredom, and so much more. Even though only a small percent of us will finish our days like this, we fear even the possibility of such a future.

Is it possible to prepare for an old age that is useful and rewarding to ourselves, our families, and our society? Can we have not only a good second half of life, but also a good death as well? These were some of the questions fueling my personal quest, questions that also helped produce this book.

Fears at Forty

As a nation we adulate youth. It dominates our ideas of the "good life." Looking and acting young, we are told, is to be valued more than anything else. This adulation tells us that there must be something "bad" about getting older, as though the process is unnatural. Women sometimes fear the process of menopause and see it as part of the whole unpleasant process of getting old. People (and sometimes the medical profession) treat aging as the enemy—to be subdued—and so denial of the aging process becomes an expensive way of life. As a society we spend thousands, millions on anti-aging procedures. It is a seductive trap.

Using large portions of our energy and time in such ways will eventually sabotage us, stealing the very resources we need to explore what it means to age successfully. Often we focus too much attention on our bodies, and we miss the larger picture of who we *really* are—spiritually, mentally, emotionally. Unsuspecting, with our priorities askew, we can easily and gradually slip onto an unrewarding and eventually futile path.

Over half a century ago, Carl Jung decried the absence of preparation for those who are entering the second half of life. He found that most people enter life after forty with the false assumption that the values, truths, and ideals that had served them adequately so far will continue to do so. Because of this false assumption, people make choices in the second half of life that invite unhappiness—and also make them difficult to be with. Jung chose harsh words to describe people caught in this negative process: hypochondriacs, niggards, doctrinaires, applauders of the past, and eternal adolescents, to name a few.

When Is Midlife?

In my business as a midlife consultant, one of the first questions people often ask me is, "When is midlife?" They seek a definition of the age range that constitutes midlife, or the middle years. I respond at a different level: "Midlife happens when it happens. . . . " I speak of midlife in terms of its

7

psychological and spiritual demands, in terms of maturity and life's landmark events. I avoid reducing midlife to a certain number of years. Passing years determine only how long a person has lived; they do not represent *how* that person has lived.

Researchers do not agree on the age range that constitutes midlife. Some assign ages forty to sixty as midlife; some include ages thirty-five up to seventy.

When I say "Midlife happens when it happens," I am trying to convey that there are certain awarenesses, recognitions, and shifts in mind, body, and spirit that seek to emerge in the middle of one's lifespan. For some, these develop in their thirties; others seem to pass through their thirties and forties uninitiated into the call of new tasks, only to be confronted when they reach their fifties or sixties. I was fifty before I really let myself feel the pain of knowing I was mortal—on a feeling level—and that my life on this earth would come to an end. Only then could I open positively to the new responsibilities and perspectives that wanted to come forth.

To enter the spirit of the middle years means that one must have accomplished certain things and have met certain requirements—prerequisites for the next stage. The challenging and potentially rewarding tasks of the middle years cannot come to those who are stuck at some earlier developmental stage, such as in adolescent values and goals. Our developmental process is influenced by how we have reacted to all that has gone before: our childhood, adolescence, and adult past. These experiences have shaped and molded what we are today.

Our development is also deeply influenced by our bodies and their physical changes in appearance and functioning.

8

We can remember how our maturing bodies affected our childhood and teen years (often embarrassingly!). In midlife also we are confronted with the inevitable fact that our bodies are changing; they are no longer as reliable and as resilient as they used to be. Women know that menopause and loss of reproductivity faces them. Our natural response to all this may be fear and denial.

I notice that in my own life and in the lives of friends, colleagues, and workshop participants there is a palpable resistance to looking ahead and admitting that we are getting older, that if we continue to live we will all someday be forty-one, fifty-five, seventy-three, ninety. I notice that the forty-year mark seems to be especially painful for many. There is an assault on the image of our youthful selves that propels us into the painful awareness of aging. Many still look remarkably young—but they can no longer successfully ignore the inroads of time.

Some speak of fears centered around their physical prowess. For some, a malaise comes unbidden and their careers no longer bring the same meaning and vitality. People in midlife often feel squeezed between the younger generation's demands and the older generation's increasing dependency. Some fear looking older, watching as wrinkles encroach, hair thins, and body shape sags. Meanwhile, their children are maturing, wearing youth like a glow around them. This serves only to accentuate inner feelings of loss of youth and beauty.

Jan, a forty-year-old woman who was attending one of my workshops, spoke of getting her eyes checked and being told that the time had come for bifocals. Jan told us that it had felt like someone had punched her in the stomach. She associated bifocals with old age; surely she was not that old!

9

Tears stung her eyes. To make matters worse, the lovely and competent twenty-two-year-old lab technician fitting the glasses condescendingly tried to soothe her.

This natural resistance to the realities of time passing can become a way of life. When we focus exclusively on beating the time clock, we squander vital energies needed to negotiate the tasks of the middle years with elegance and courage—energies needed to create a future rich with rewards.

A Realistic Assessment— The Choice Is Ours

Successful aging begins with a realistic assessment of our life situation and the challenges that will undoubtedly confront us. We can choose to meet our futures more fully prepared. The choice not to choose means that we choose to live irresponsibly. If we do not select our activities and attitudes with clear judgment coming from a courageous and realistic assessment of our lives and circumstances, we fall into poor unconscious choices. We usually choose what seems easiest and most comfortable in the moment, not realizing the terrible price we will pay later on.

We are always making choices, whether we realize it or not. Responsible choosing envisions the consequences that will follow each choice. It requires that we take time to reflect. In projecting the outcomes of our current ways of life we should ask ourselves:

- What will probably happen if I continue this path?
- Is that what I really want for myself?
- Am I ready to accept the consequences of what I am choosing, for both myself and others?

10

Through such a reasoned and responsible choice process, combined with careful listening to our intuition and insights, we can contribute to a fulfilling future—for ourselves and for those around us. Although we have incredible power to forge our destinies, outside influences invade our lives. At such times, our power lies in our ability to choose our responses. We are both the potter and the clay. When we are the potter, we have the opportunity to shape our clay-self. When we are the clay, we can choose creative acceptance with the student's mind: "What am I to learn in all this?" Or, we can resist and feel defensive and victimized: "How could this happen to me?" Our power of choice lies in assessing our particular situation and learning to use whatever is happening for our long-term benefit.

Cultivating the creative attitude can change everything. Conscious choosing like this will take work. Sometimes the way of wisdom means we seek counsel.

Recognizing the need for change and then following through with that change is not easy. One prerequisite to positive change is the willingness to face the truth about life—and about our own life in particular. Facing the truth includes recognizing our fears of the future.

Fear as the First Motivator for Change

Daring to realistically assess where we are in the life span takes courage. Before we gain this courage, we must pass through the ordeal of acknowledging our fears about the future. Fear makes us feel helpless and can be a barrier to choosing well.

During an exercise in a group discussion I led, we all imagined ourselves ten years older. In the middle of the

11

session, Kurt, a man of forty, abruptly left the room. Later he explained that the idea of turning fifty made him sick to his stomach. He was struggling just to accept being forty and it was impossible for him to imagine being fifty without feeling physically ill. Kurt could use this experience as a way of accepting his fear of aging.

Some questions he might ask himself: "Why did I become so afraid when imagining myself ten years older?" "What do I think of people in their fifties?" "What can I do right now to make it safer for me to consider my future in five years, or in ten years?" "How are my parents aging?" "Are my attitudes toward their process contributing to my feelings?" "Do I know anyone from the older generation that I could admire and accept as a model?"

Zanya, a lovely artist in her early forties, tried to imagine herself in ten years. But as she pondered an image of an older, wiser self, it was interrupted by an image of her mother. Zanya was visibly angered by this unexpected vision. One of her fears for her future centered around her mother—she did not want to repeat her mother's aging pattern. Zanya's experience shows us it's important to understand and study our close relationships, particularly those of our childhood family. If we are not aware of these lives and dynamics, we tend to repeat them, mistakes and all.

Kurt and Zanya illustrate that the journey into realistically assessing where one is in the life span takes honesty and perseverance. To move beyond our fears we dare not ignore them, but begin to recognize and accept them. Fear of aging is justified because of the obstacles to be negotiated —it is easy to get on a negative track. Our fears, however, can serve as a healthy motivating force that stimulates us to begin the work of necessary changes.

12

Facing the Truth—Useful Pain

Truth by its nature is empowering. Avoiding the truth sabotages us because we then make decisions based on illusion. The essential nature of truth brings light, awareness, honesty, health. These are the building blocks for successfully living the second half of life.

The truth always points us in the direction of freedom. Using our fears as a beacon calling us to the truth helps us cut through our resistances. We can then gradually uncover and let go of any false assumptions and securities we have adopted. Anything false will always let us down, preventing us from discovering our true desires.

Facing the truth about the life we have lived so far and the life we are living today is a necessary midlife task on the way to a richly rewarding second half of life.

In Anthony de Mello's book of parables and stories, *Song of the Bird,* is a story titled "The Truth Shop."

> I could hardly believe my eyes when I saw the name of the shop: THE TRUTH SHOP. The saleswoman was very polite: What type of truth did I wish to purchase, partial or whole? The whole truth, of course. No deceptions for me, no defenses, no rationalizations. I wanted my truth plain and unadulterated. She waved me on to another side of the store.
>
> The salesman there pointed to the price tag. "The price is very high, sir," he said. "What is it?" I asked, determined to get the whole truth, no matter what it cost. "Your security, sir," he answered.
>
> I came away with a heavy heart.
>
> I still need the safety of my unquestioned beliefs.

Seeking the truth about ourselves also includes a willingness to allow ourselves to be changed. Only by releasing the old ways, and enduring the loss of former behaviors and attitudes, can we then make room for new ways.

Changing Directions:
Two Roads into the Second Half of Life

The famous character Scrooge, in Charles Dickens's *A Christmas Carol,* is the quintessential example of a person who changed directions when he faced his fears and allowed the truth of his past to free him.

The enormous popularity of Dickens's tale of human transformation indicates that it touches a deep chord in all of us. Scrooge's situation, before and after his transformation, can be likened to two roads in life, each with very different destinations. Both roads contain pitfalls and possible detours, but if we journey along the self-absorbed road, we fail to climb out of the pits or to recover from the detours and instead sink into an escalating concern with our own life, which becomes more narrow and irrelevant. We focus on what we eat and wear, how we feel, how we pass the time and entertain ourselves, how offended we are by perceived slights from others, how much we blame others for our problems, how much we demand attention from others, how sorry we feel about our lot in life, and so on.

When we choose the path of self-absorption we find our world constricting until, as one physician observed from his practice, our lives are focused on what goes into our bodies and what comes out of them. If we fall into such traps (and it is so easy to do), we feel increasingly unhappy and useless.

The road that Scrooge took calls for a new birth to a new way of being. Midlife—or any major transition in life—is a time for change, a time to give birth to our future and the quality of that future. We can deny the passing of time, we can delay our developmental tasks, but mercifully they will not leave us alone and will continue to call to us throughout life.

When we travel on this road of new birth, the road leading to successful aging, we start by wondering who we really are and why we are here. Cosmic questions regarding the meaning of life force their way into our awareness. Everything comes up for inspection. Activities that once brought meaning and rewards lose their vitality.

This intense questioning period can be disorienting. We find ourselves asking, "What is it I really want and need to do?" "What gives me energy?" "What do I need to clear from my life to make room for what I really must do?" "What will it cost?" "What are my deepest values that I want to honor?" "Are there interests and skills I want to develop?"

When we engage in this process of questioning and sorting out we begin to take more responsibility for how our daily choices affect our future and the future of others. Perhaps, for example, we become more concerned about the needs of the planet and seek opportunities for thoughtful service. Our personalities expand to include others in our thoughts, energies, and love. This helps keep life in perspective, enabling us to transcend many everyday irritations with a balancing peace and joy.

Our resistances to the changes that are called for in the second half of life can be formidable and may have roots deep in our family patterns. How our parents, grandparents, and great-grandparents handled their lives and aging processes influences us. Cultural anthropologist and author Angeles Arrien spoke of the combined wisdom that comes to us from indigenous peoples around the world. They feel that the ancestors are watching each one of us, very interested

15

in our choices—in our life direction. The old ones stand by our shoulders and whisper amongst themselves: "Oh, maybe this will be the one who will break the harmful family patterns; maybe this one will bring forth the good medicine in our family line—the loving, the true, and beautiful —to gift mother earth."

If we do break negative family patterns, we should be prepared to overcome the guilt that may emerge if we claim for ourselves a new and better way. Experiencing our anxiety and taking the time to listen to ourselves with compassion invites a positive change.

Taking a new path can encourage the blossoming of our higher potential, helping us to avoid the dead-end of self-absorption and stagnation, components of unsuccessful maturing. Moving beyond our fears puts us in touch with our inner power, and we assess our life choices with greater truthfulness, clarity, and potency. We are freer to choose the positive path leading to an abundant future.

CHAPTER TWO

Growing Older Richly— Through All Life's Stages

I went to the woods because I wished to live deliberately, to front only the essential facts of life, and see if I could not learn what it had to teach, and not, when I came to die, to discover that I had not lived.

—HENRY DAVID THOREAU

TO UNDERSTAND MORE CLEARLY what is meant by successful aging, we need to gain perspective on successful living. The work of Erik Erikson, one of the most influential developmental psychologists of our time, provides us with a model. In the 1950s he first proposed that development occurs throughout our entire life span. Psychologists and educators had accepted that children passed through developmental stages, but the theories seemed to stop there. Somehow at age twenty-one we were supposed to emerge out of childhood fully formed with generous qualities of wisdom, love, and integrity to manage the rest of our lives.

Erikson, a keen thinker and observer of life, noticed that human growth seems to occur in certain sequential segments over one's entire life span. Each segment has specific tasks that can be negotiated successfully or unsuccessfully. Whatever the outcome, the results have significant impact on an individual's future.

Erikson came to the field of psychology from the field of art, so his work was enhanced by the artist's ability to see deeply into life. His theories are grounded in what he observed to be the essential realities of being human.

In developing the concept that human life unfolds in an orderly manner, Erikson and others uncovered some key principles. Each stage of human development contains new hopes and new responsibilities—and also new pitfalls. The way we move through the stages and their specific tasks affects our future: either we move on or we regress.

Each succeeding stage builds on the previous ones; we cannot skip over them. When something is amiss, our development can be stunted or distorted, but we can go back and reclaim missing elements at a later time. Reclaiming a missing piece influences our entire development, past and future.

A new stage is often introduced by a crisis or a marker event in our external lives, like marriage, the birth of a child, job change or loss, death of a loved one, divorce, sickness, accident. Sometimes the pressure that upsets our usual patterns and heralds a change comes from our inner lives instead. We find new questions emerging, new awarenesses, or perhaps a depression.

As with most change, we endure a time of instability while the new challenges unfold. Because the challenges of each transition period are often a little more than we can master easily, we face a time of both vulnerability and potential. Successful negotiation of the tasks inherent in each stage contributes new strengths and resources to our personalities. This prepares the way for higher and still-developing powers.

Although this book concentrates on the second half of life, obviously we cannot discuss it separately from the first half. How we reacted to the events and people that filled our childhoods and young adult lives is crucial to who we are today.

Our little child of yesterday, who lives deep within us, holds the secret to our creativity and the keys to our future. (Chapter eleven deals with this important topic in more depth.) Midlife is often a time to recognize the little child's needs, a time to go back and reclaim wounded and missing pieces from the first part of life.

When we return to reclaim missing pieces or when we move to the next developmental stage, the additions are not just layered on top of what we already are, like putting on a coat. Instead, everything in our developmental journey interconnects—when one piece is added or shifted, a new cloth is woven.

Shaping our lives is like making a flavorful soup. The pot has been simmering on the back burner for some time. The chef (that's you!) tastes the concoction, chooses to add an ingredient—a spice, a broth, a bit of wine—and suddenly the whole creation changes to a different flavor. The same with our lives; we do the work of reclaiming a missing piece or we add a flavorful ingredient and the essence is changed.

We come into the world with tremendous assets—great resources for creative self-expression and self-healing. We are more than we know. We are fully equipped to accomplish our deeply held life goals. We can count on this!

Five Stages of Childhood

To better understand the choices we are facing in the second half of life, let's explore in more detail some of the main points of Erikson's human development theory, beginning with infancy. From his observations in various settings and cultures, Erikson composed an eight-stage developmental theory—five are concerned with childhood and three with adulthood. Each stage is concerned with a lesson or task to be completed in order to gain useful strengths.

Stage One. In infancy the first task to be negotiated is *trust vs. mistrust.* Infants need to receive a quality of care that encourages development of a sense of trustworthiness and meaning. This gives them a basic sense of trust in themselves and in the goodness of their environment. The strength or resource that comes with trust is *hope,* which is a capacity of expectant desire. If infants are not cared for well, they may develop a fundamental mistrust of themselves and others that could last a lifetime, sabotaging the work and rewards of the later stages.

Stage Two. Early childhood brings the task of *autonomy vs. shame and doubt.* Here children begin to experiment with holding on and letting go. Their muscles begin to mature and they can assert their autonomy. If their battles with those who are bigger and stronger end in constant defeat, they fail to learn about their developing will. Instead they develop a deep sense of doubt and shame. On the other hand, if a sense of autonomy is fostered, they will gain a quality of self-esteem that includes a sense of goodwill, personal dignity, and lawful independence. The resource gained in successfully passing through this stage is *will,* a rudimentary power of free choice and self-restraint.

20

Stage Three. The "play" age brings *initiative vs. guilt.* Here children can move around and communicate with increasing freedom. They are stimulated to develop their imaginations. Initiative adds to autonomy (Stage Two) the quality of planning and undertaking something. With their surplus of energy, children forget failures quickly and move on with renewed motivation. However, their activities, curiosity, and fantasies can lead to feelings of guilt and anxiety if these natural tendencies are overlayed too heavily with adult interferences and burdens. Children may then decide that they are essentially bad. The burden of being bad can block initiative or even reduce a child to display retaliation and vindictiveness. The strength or virtue developed in this stage is *purpose,* the faculty of intending and designing.

Stage Four. School age brings *industry vs. inferiority.* Now children begin to learn to accept teachings and teachers and how to perform and make things that win recognition from others. This is the time to develop the capacity to enjoy work. A child needs to gain positive recognition by working on projects and bringing them to completion. When children do not receive affirmation for work accomplished, there is the danger of a growing sense of inadequacy and inferiority. The strength of this stage is *competence,* the ability to master the tasks of life with skill and sufficiency.

Stage Five. Adolescence is the time for *identity vs. identity diffusion.* Puberty, rapid body growth, and sexual maturing bring a time of questioning and rebellion. Childhood comes to an end. Values and ideas that had been accepted and relied on now come under fire. The difficult task facing adolescents is to integrate their newly emerging biological drives, social roles, and inborn talents with their accumulated experiences. Adolescents fall in love easily—attempting

21

to learn about themselves by projecting parts of their unknown self onto others, gradually clarifying their individual identity. Adolescents can be cliquish, eager to be accepted by their peers, and cruel in their exclusion of all who are different. They test others in their circles to see if they are loyal. The virtue gained when this stage is successfully negotiated is *fidelity,* the ability to be faithful, to be true.

Young adults, hopefully, have been able to partially accomplish the developmental tasks of childhood and have gained at least a modest amount of childhood's five strengths: hope, will, purpose, competence, and fidelity. These will be essential in order to take on the challenges of adulthood with vigor and confidence.

Three Stages of Adulthood

Erikson divided adulthood into early, middle, and late stages, each with specific tasks and strengths.

Stage Six. Young adulthood is the time to choose *intimacy vs. isolation.* To feel secure enough to reach out to others and struggle with intimacy's tasks, young adults must first be intimate with themselves and with their inner lives. This intimacy gives them the foundation from which to reach out to others in a healthy way.

Intimacy is the capacity to commit oneself to others. The quality of commitment or partnership calls for the ability to make sacrifices, compromises, and needed adaptations to another over time. The virtue or strength gained is *love,* a kind of love inspired by dreams of what one can do and care for with another. Those who are unable to enter wholeheartedly into emotionally close alliances may develop a sense of

22

isolation. They may be too handicapped to negotiate the next stage of adulthood well, failing therefore to reap its benefits.

Stage Seven. Adulthood presents the challenge of *generativity vs. self-absorption and stagnation.* Out of the maturing intimacies of early adulthood grows an ability to care for others and the environment, which can be passed on to younger generations. The word chosen to describe this phenomenon is "generativity." Erikson hoped this word would be useful in conveying the deep, instinctual, generative roots behind the energy that calls us to continue our development through the adult years. This is a time to be concerned with maintaining the world.

If generativity is not developed, we may fall into self-absorption and stagnation, thus missing the opportunity to contribute to the lives of others. To fail at generativity is to fail to be able to give in a self-fulfilling way to the needs of the earth, and its people. The resource of personality that emerges with maturing generativity is *care,* the ability to protect, to care for, to be vigilant.

Stage Eight. Old age, the late period of adulthood, challenges individuals with the task of *integrity vs. despair.* When we have achieved satisfying relationships with others and have adapted to both the joys and losses that come out of our generative activities, we can count on an unshakable sense of integrity. Such integrity comes from making whole the confusing and separate parts of ourselves. We enjoy a feeling of dignity, we deeply affirm who we are. This sense of personal value holds firm in spite of physical and economic threats. The virtue gained is *wisdom.* This wisdom includes the ability to understand and discern; it includes an enlargement of mind, a far-sightedness.

If we fail to negotiate these stages of our lives positively, we will experience despair because our time left is so short. We will be unable to take comfort in the fact that we have accomplished what was essential for us, and we will fear death.

But My Life Doesn't Fit This Theory

Theories about human behavior are not meant to be complete truths, but useful guides. Theories can provide maps of the territory we call adulthood and can help us predict and describe patterns of behavior as well as understand and interpret them. There is not one perfect theory that will fit for everyone. In fact, there is a lot of ambiguity. Our task is to select what is useful and set the rest aside.

Many of us have had childhoods in which traumatic events, parental inadequacies, or other circumstances stunted or inhibited our growth in certain ways. In my own life I was not able to accomplish the first task of the infant—cultivation of trust. Nor did I acquire hope, the strength of this stage.

I entered adulthood with a pervading sense of mistrust in myself and my world. I was like Chicken Little in the children's story who thought the sky was falling. Because I had not gained an adequate amount of the resource hope, which infants receive when they are in trustworthy environments, I had a nagging distrust of the future and wondered what horrible things might happen next. I was not able to engage in healthy relationships; I believed in a God who would punish; I was sick a lot; I was excessively burdened. Trying valiantly to overcome everything, I judged myself harshly for my inability to be happier and more loving.

I increasingly became aware of a need to seek help because of the mistakes I made, realizing that my handicaps

24

were affecting my children. My task, which I finally accepted wholeheartedly in my forties, was to pick up that lost piece—and other lost pieces—of my developmental journey. I deliberately chose to enter into activities that could help me, such as reading, group work, therapy, educational strategies, spiritual seeking, and more.

Nothing is fixed or unchangeable about our development —that is the good news! Also, the tempo, intensity, and mastery of the developmental journey differs widely for each individual. Each of us has a different set of influences and circumstances to contend with, and we also have great strengths and resources within us to accomplish our goals.

When we fail to address the issues that matter deeply to us we devalue ourselves and end up feeling angry, depressed, or victimized. Successful aging is a process that will take commitment, but unsuccessful aging will steal our birthright—the opportunity to make a fulfilling and rewarding contribution.

Midlife—A Crucial Time for Many

In midlife we see that we are called upon to move forward toward our highest potential. This entry into midlife can take one by surprise, as it did author Judith Viorst:

What am I doing with a midlife crisis?
This morning I was seventeen.
I have barely begun the beguine and it's
Good-night ladies
Already.

While I've been wondering who to be
When I grow up someday,
My acne has vanished away and it's

Sagging kneecaps
Already.

Why do I seem to remember Pearl Harbor?
Surely, I must be too young.
When did the boys I once clung to
Start losing their hair?

Why can't I take barefoot walks in the park
Without giving my kidneys a chill?
There's poetry left in me still and it
Doesn't seem fair.

While I was thinking I was just a girl
My future turned into my past.
The time for wild kisses goes fast and it's
Time for Sanka.
Already?

The task of the midlife developmental transition is to make peace with the past and prepare for the future. We begin to cultivate the time for reflection; every aspect of our lives comes up for inspection and the neglected parts of ourselves urgently seek expression. This is the time to examine long-held assumptions about life and the world and see if they stand up under the scrutiny of a more tested and mature perspective.

Those who emphasize the social aspects of midlife speak in terms of interactions with family, career, and society, when life's responsibilities are at their peak and society's expectations are often unrealistic. Many experience intense striving to succeed in work and career in the middle years while there is still time.

If career goals have been reached, people often ask whether all that effort was worth it, and if this is "really all there is." In the middle years one often deals on the one hand with children who have unrealistic expectations about their parents and on the other hand with aging parents who are becoming demanding, frail, or in need of help. In between these two generations is one's self and one's own needs, hopes, and fears.

Midlife brings with it an invitation to accept ourselves as we truly are, embracing the darker sides of ourselves as well as the good, the dark sides of our cultures as well as the good. We have an instinctive fear of facing the dark mysteries. The shadow or unknown parts of us belong to an inner world that is usually suppressed in the first half of life. We tend to hang on to the childish belief that maybe there is no death or evil in the world. We like to feel we're special, that there is a magical safety net to protect us from disaster. But by confronting our mysterious and shadowy center, we tap into life's revitalizing energies and gain access to our innermost self, which contains the key to a new understanding of our life's meaning.

Carl Jung, acknowledged by many to be the father of the study of adult development, saw the transition of midlife as a genuine spiritual crisis. He saw life in two stages, the first half and the second half, with midlife as the pivotal time between. Jung stated that in midlife we need to redirect the energy we used to gain a place in the outer world, that our energy now should be used to search out new meaning. If we accomplish this task, a renaissance emerges, and we connect to our true selves.

Generativity in the Middle Years

"Generativity" means giving birth to the new aspects of ourselves that will assure a higher sense of well-being in the middle years and beyond. It means finding new and practical ways of caring for those who come after us and for the quality of social systems and environment that is passed on to them. The path of generativity helps us to avoid the dangers of self-absorption and stagnation because we learn to live in new ways that expand our horizons.

Generativity is a process whereby we learn to follow our deeper interests and longings. We find ways to reach out— perhaps we are attracted to help end world hunger or to promote better family dynamics or to provide loving care for the dying. We may enjoy becoming involved in politics, recycling waste, eliminating violence on TV, humanizing the corrections systems, or stopping child abuse. We become involved not only because these things need attention, but because we reap incredible rewards when we make contributions.

The middle years are generally the time when personal power is at its highest, caring responsibilities are at their fullest, and we feel the insistent urge to take time to reflect. Creative midlife is an attitude to be cultivated, a way of being that is vital, concerned, empowering. Some people retain the vigor and zest associated with the middle years through their sixties, seventies, eighties—on to the end of their days. This is the model that beckons to me as I study successful aging and its characteristics.

Findings from My Studies

I interviewed in depth middle-aged women and men who were highly generative, and who had discovered unique ways to give to others. I subsequently worked with Chicago's Market Facts, Inc. to conduct a national survey of close to six hundred people ages forty to seventy-five who filled out questionnaires concerning their experiences of the second half of their lives.

From these studies I was able to better understand and clarify some qualities of generative people. I share these with you.

Successful Aging

People who are maturing positively have these attributes:

1. They have evolved a generous view of others and of the world, which includes maintaining a forgiving stance toward faults and inadequacies in themselves and others.
2. They have a giving attitude toward themselves and others. They give more financially than do most people.
3. They form a caring and positive relationship with nature. They are concerned about the quality of the environment that will be passed on to future generations.
4. They are reflective and seek self-understanding.
5. They have had a pivotal event or events that led to transition or re-birth experiences. Everyone has such events, but generative people use them to grow and expand while non-generative people withdraw and blame others for their misfortunes.
6. They simplify their lives. Generative people take time to gain the insights needed to clear away clutter and confusion. They learn to set limits.
7. They have the courage to change both themselves and conditions around them.
8. They describe themselves as spiritual. They trust God or some Higher Power, and they trust the life process.

9. They are sought out by others for counsel, wisdom, perspective, and creative insight.
10. They are committed to continued learning. Generative people often spend considerable time learning on their own or attend a variety of workshops and classes.
11. They are clearly engaged in caring behaviors toward themselves and others.
12. They are evolving healthier eating and exercise patterns.
13. They find laughter and tears coming easily and spontaneously.
14. They are hopeful people. They take their dreams seriously, and their lives demonstrate that some dreams do come true.
15. They have the courage to deal with their own mortality, making appropriate plans as needed.

Unsuccessful Aging

Those caught in self-absorption and stagnation will increasingly manifest such personality characteristics as:

1. A tendency to blame others for problems, and feelings of isolation.
2. A tendency to alienate other people. Those aging unsuccessfully are difficult to be with for more than a brief time.
3. Moodiness, irritability, thoughtlessness, low vitality, chronic anger, despair, meanness of spirit.
4. Clinging to rigid opinions, unable to set them aside long enough to listen to another's views or experiences. They don't allow certain people or topics to be

mentioned and those around them are careful not to share delicate or intimate subjects.

5. An inability to enjoy and adapt to the changing world.
6. A need to hang on to money.
7. An increasing obsession with life's inequities and their own wounds.
8. A noticeable lack of intimate friends of any generation.
9. A high use of alcohol, tranquilizers, or other forms of escape, such as TV, frenetic activity, etc.
10. The inability to be a "wise elder," who has something of lasting value to give to others.
11. A tendency to create guilty feelings in those around them.
12. An excessive focus on themselves, especially on their health problems and body functions.
13. Fears of the future.

Naturally enough, we all have a mixture of qualities from both lists. But what we want to do is increasingly cultivate the generative behaviors that have long-range benefits leading to high life satisfaction for ourselves and others.

Considering Long-Range Benefits

Creative aging requires that we think ahead and consider the long-term effects of our daily choices. As we develop the ability to listen to our deeper Self, we begin to recognize what will enhance our lives and what will hurt or even destroy us.

Let me illustrate a fork in the road for me—a time when I had to evaluate the consequences of choosing a short-term pleasure with destructive overtones. Although it started

31

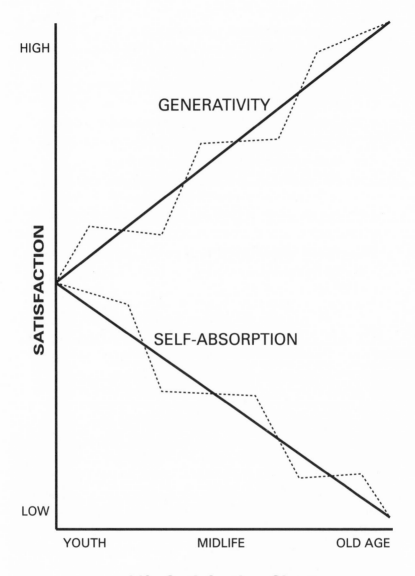

Life Satisfaction Chart

innocently, the path I chose could have led to long-term unhappiness and despair.

CHANGING A DESTRUCTIVE RITUAL
TO A POSITIVE ONE

My husband, David, and I (both in our fifties at the time) had not been married very long and had both been married before. During the time we dated, we had dinner out with friends or by ourselves two or three times a week. We became accustomed to having a drink together before dinner, and in time, the before-dinner drinks became a ritual that we carried into our marriage.

After marriage and my moving into his house, we had lots of challenges as we attempted to bring together a blended family. We developed a pattern: after our day's activities, as I started dinner David frosted some long-stemmed glasses. Then he ceremoniously mixed his favorite alcoholic concoction and poured the color-ful liquid into the waiting frosty crystal. It was good to look at, lovely to taste, and promised a warm glow. We then moved to the living room to discuss our family and share the events of the day. As people who were try-ing to blend together two families, we had much to dis-cuss. It was also a chance to share time together alone. Our cocktail time quickly became an essential ritual.

Soon, however, I found that I wanted another drink and even another. Our quiet, intimate moments turned into arguments a few times and then, one night, into a real battle. Those alcohol-influenced fights solved none of our problems and only intensified the trouble.

Clearly we needed to change; we talked about our ritual and what it was doing to us. Although it was time set aside just for us, we were not using it well. We realized we wanted to keep the sense of sharing and working together. I felt cared for as David worked in the kitchen with me.

However, there were the undesired side effects of alcohol—the overload of sugary calories, the loss of control when we had a disagreement. I did not want to slide into alcohol dependency, a fear that lurked in the back of my mind. The abuse of alcohol in my former family was a specter I knew only too well. Our challenge was to find something that would give us the good parts of our ritual while avoiding the negative ones.

We hit on a solution that proved incredibly rewarding. I had always wanted to do more walking, but had never taken my desire seriously. Why couldn't we make walking together our new, healthier ritual. David agreed to give it a try. We bought good walking shoes. Then, with his mathematical tendencies, David drove the car around the neighborhood to plot a two-mile course. Walking quickly became our ritual. We'd get into our comfy clothes and walk, sharing the day's events. We didn't give up alcohol, but we changed a dangerous ritual.

This choice led to others (they always do!). For our next vacation we decided to go someplace where we could walk a bit. We decided on Colorado and enjoyed taking three- or four-mile hikes in the mountains. On one excursion partway up Longs Peak, we were congratulating ourselves for our physical prowess (at our age!) as, huffing and puffing, we rounded a bend in the upward trail. Coming toward us at a fast clip was a small, energetic woman muttering to herself. Seeing us, she just naturally included us in her conversation:

"That's just like him! He has to climb to the top and he's eighty-two years old. I'm so furious at him. He just won't listen to me! I had to turn around and I'm only seventy-six. It'll be the death of him. Are you on your way up?"

"Well . . ." we stalled, our words of self-congratulation drying up in our mouths. "Well, we're going up a little farther."

"You must tell him I couldn't keep up with him and I'll meet him at the waterfall. Tell him I'm mad at him; it's time for him to act his age!"

At this point she broke out in a smile and said in a very different tone, "He's just wonderful. We have so much fun together, but sometimes he just has to show off . . ." David and I felt that we had been shown a rich example of successful aging, something that was possible for us. It seemed that our choice to walk began to have a life of its own. We walked with renewed vigor. We began seeking out forest preserves for longer Saturday walks, and we urged ourselves to do the fifteen-minute mile or four miles an hour on flat terrain.

On our vacation a year later, we went to England, famous for its interesting walking trails. In the Lake District, we tackled seven- and eight-mile walks, always surprised at how many older people were walking. We enjoyed our new understanding of what people our age and beyond could do.

I had a cherished dream about seeing the Himalayas. I did not tell David, or anyone else, about my dream. It seemed too exotic, too tender. Then one day at a little Thai restaurant near the campus where I was a graduate student I overheard a young couple and their Nepalese friend talking about their experiences of trekking

35

in the Himalayas. I eavesdropped until I couldn't stand it another minute and joined them, bursting with questions: Where? How? Who? When? The Nepalese student, a man in his thirties, invited me to his home to meet his wife and family and to show me slides of Nepal and the Himalayas. I couldn't believe my good fortune. It was almost as if my little dream began to have a life of its own, attracting into my life the elements to realize it.

David thought I was crazy. "What's the matter with Paris?" was his response. Then we went cross-country skiing with two couples who are very close friends. Later in the evening I spoke of my dream. Two of them did not think I was crazy; in fact, they were intrigued. One with a particularly adventurous spirit remembered friends who had gone to the Himalayas, and decided to contact them.

All sorts of "coincidences" continued to develop until nine months later a motley group of six Americans in their fifties and early sixties arrived at the trailhead in Gorka, Nepal. We definitely were not the "jock" type. Some of us were overweight. Some had worked too hard and were tired. But we were daring, risking—and scared!

The five-mile-high, magical, mystical mountains towered over us, resplendent in their snowy jackets of reflected pinks, oranges, creams, blues, and mauves. They were breathtaking (maybe part of that was altitude!). The clouds and mists would close over them in moments, and we would wait with anticipation, hoping that they would unveil themselves again.

We had guides, cooks, porters, the whole works for a full-fledged ten-day trek. And, it costs about the same to have all the equipment, food, service, and guidance per day as it does to stay in an average motel in the United

36

States. There was one financial hitch, the air fare getting there was a challenge!

Another hitch—daring to dream the dream. We changed our priorities from sitting home after work and drinking to an activity that contributed to our excitement, health, and well-being. The short-term pleasure of another pretty drink was laid aside for the long-term benefit of beginning to walk, to use our bodies, to train, to go for an as-yet unrecognized dream. One surprise element was how much life seemed to conspire on behalf of the dream, turning up the right people at the right time, quieting our fears, encouraging us just when we thought it was impossible.

David and I learned the lesson that one choice leads to another and then another. As Robert Frost wrote, "Way leads on to way." I often think of that phrase "the choice is always ours." Can we dare to believe we have that much power over our lives and futures?

Daring to Disturb Your Life

By keeping in mind that short-term relief often leads to long-term cost, we can help to motivate ourselves to negotiate needed changes. Short-term pleasures are just that—short and quick. They are easy and do not build the strength needed to handle life's stresses and challenges. Short-term pleasures can sabotage our self-worth; they do not lead to involvement in life, but in the opposite direction, toward escaping life's demands. They do not build character, but tend to dull one's vitality.

Long-term enjoyments often take work and demand effort at times when we would rather not work so hard. Challenging interests open the gate to internal strengths

37

and we gain a sense of competency, increased self-confidence and self-esteem. The good feelings last and the sense of fulfillment is unshakable.

The costs of change are high, but the costs of not changing may be higher. When change is called for and we refuse to engage in it, we sacrifice the Self, the most desirable inner core, and sentence ourselves and others to suffer needlessly.

If we already are disturbed about where our lives are going, we need to be gentle and patient with ourselves. As the poet Rainer Maria Rilke advised a young writer who was lost in questions and doubt, we need to try to accept that which is unsolved in our hearts and love even our questions.

If you are heading in a direction that will prove unrewarding, even dangerous, as I was, it is good that you find yourself disturbed, for that is the beginning of change. You will eventually also come to feel the love behind your feelings of disturbance. Someone once said, "God disturbs the comfortable and comforts the disturbed."

CHAPTER THREE

Choices, Changes, More Choices

Lord grant me the serenity
To accept the things I cannot change
The courage to change the things I can
And the wisdom to know the difference.

—SERENITY PRAYER

THE POET ROBERT FROST understood much about the power, process, and implications of choice in our lives. Often read and quoted, Frost's poem "The Road Not Taken" catches something of the dilemma we face as we consider various paths or options in the way ahead.

Two roads diverged in a yellow wood,
And sorry I could not travel both
And be one traveler, long I stood
And looked down one as far as I could
To where it bent in the undergrowth;

Then took the other, as just as fair,
And having perhaps the better claim,

Because it was grassy and wanted wear;
Though as for that the passing there
Had worn them really about the same,

And both that morning equally lay
In leaves no step had trodden black.
Oh, I kept the first for another day!
Yet knowing how way leads on to way,
I doubted if I should ever come back.

I shall be telling this with a sigh
Somewhere ages and ages hence:
Two roads diverged in a wood, and I—
I took the one less traveled by,
And that has made all the difference.

The early morning walker had left town, away from the noise and hurry of life, midst trees and nature. We, too, must give ourselves time alone, open spaces in our schedules to give our true needs and longings the chance to emerge. This is a prerequisite step for creative choice.

We are told it was a morning woods, a yellow woods. We can dare to imagine it was a mystical moment, as early morning is likely to be, and the whole scene must have held a numinous quality.

The traveler took some time to look ahead—and, taking that kind of time, became aware that a choice had to be made. Often we can be in such a hurry we don't even recognize a moment laden with choice. This traveler took the time to consider both paths. We can imagine the traveler craning his or her neck to get a better look—to peer just a few more feet into the possible future. Wouldn't it be nice to make our decisions after we clearly saw what we are deciding about? But like the traveler, we usually have to make them from hints, clues, partial insights.

Something called the traveler toward the path that was more grassy, less traveled—it "wanted wear." Our friend has that most human quality of wishing to have it all, and we hear the promise to come back someday and take the other one, too. Then in the next moment the traveler realizes that "way leads on to way." In taking one path, we seldom can go back and make a choice over again. We feel a certain melancholy in the choosing, wondering if the other road might have been better.

The poem closes with the traveler sensing that this decision is a major life choice, and continues the walk that is far more than a morning stroll, the walk that is a metaphor for a life journey. In looking back from the future, the traveler knows the right decision was made. The traveler separated from the crowd and took the way that was uniquely right, as we also must do.

Everyday Tasks at Different Stages

Each stage of our life journey has its own responsibilities, duties, and challenges. In adulthood, our lives are lived out in the outward everyday patterns of job, family, friends, and other responsibilities. Inner forces—desires, fears, ambitions, strivings, discouragements, questionings—also make themselves felt. And while each of us will have experiences that are uniquely our own, we will also find much that we share in common with others.

Those of you in your late thirties and early forties may find that thoughts and intimations of your own mortality begin to come to you. This emerging awareness can prove explosive to some, throwing old patterns and values into question. In this unstable time you may find yourself:

41

- Wondering what it all means
- Reevaluating your career or occupation
- Reassessing financial goals
- Preparing for a career change
- Reassessing your lifestyle, priorities, and values
- Relating to your teenage children
- Relating to your aging parents
- Reassessing the relationship with your mate
- Adjusting to divorce or remarriage
- Looking at needed change in your life—making choices
- Taking a renewed interest in physical fitness
- Rediscovering a partnership with nature
- Seriously undertaking the spiritual quest

Those of you in your middle forties and fifties may work on:

- A continued search for life's deeper meaning
- Adjusting your expectations of career or occupation
- Managing finances to insure adequate future income
- Continuing focus on quality of relationship with mate
- Fostering independence in your young adult children
- Adjusting to grandparenting
- Becoming more deeply involved in friendships
- More involvement in community concerns
- Handling increasing demands from aging parents
- Simplifying your life
- Increasing knowledge of preventive health care
- An environmentally responsible lifestyle
- Picking up lost pieces in your developmental journey
- Self-improvement—taking classes and workshops

For those of you who have moved into your late fifties and early sixties, you may find yourself doing some of these things:

- Coping with health problems, learning about health care
- Deepening your personal relationships
- Increasing your involvement with grandchildren
- Preparing to refocus your career energies
- Expanding your avocational and volunteer interests
- Financing new interests—planning financial future
- Adjusting to more constant companionship with mate or adjusting to single life
- Facing death through the death of parents or friends
- Continuing to pick up pieces of your developmental journey while reaping rewards from work already done
- Continuing to simplify your life, focusing on what is vital and right for you
- Continuing responsibility for your impact on the environment while increasingly enjoying nature
- Practicing speaking the truth as you see it
- Seeking and enjoying mentoring opportunities
- Enjoying the rewards of a spiritual quest

The late sixties, seventies, and beyond—a stage called retirement in our culture—needs to be re-thought and re-evaluated. The word "retire," for example, should be dropped from our vocabulary when referring to an age group. The meaning of the word in the *Concise Oxford Dictionary* is, "withdraw, go away, retreat, seek seclusion, recede, go (as) to bed." This, unfortunately, is our society's attitude to those in their sixties and beyond. We say, in effect, "Just go away and play now. We'll manage the world; you've become obsolete."

43

Certainly those who have kept their vitality and have lived and learned have much to give, much to share, much to do. How many of us would dearly love to have an older friend who could offer us wisdom, resources, experience, expertise, and love? How might our earlier lives have been different if we had had such a person to count on? How might our life be different today if we now had a trusted elder to go to for encouragement, perspective, and comfort? Those who have chosen the generative way of successful aging are such people, and we need them desperately. Those of you in your late sixties and beyond may be:

- Exploring creative ways to reflect on, integrate, and pass on wisdom from life experiences
- Disengaging from reliance on paychecks
- Being concerned with personal health care
- Adjusting to physical limitations
- Searching for and enjoying new achievement outlets
- Adjusting to deaths of loved ones and friends
- Intentionally cultivating new relationships
- Enjoying grandchildren growing up
- Accepting the naturalness of physical death and preparing for the mystery of what comes next
- Putting affairs in order
- Making suitable living arrangements
- Finding nature a solace, an ever-present friend
- Kindly speaking the truth as you see and understand it
- Enjoying mentoring
- Seeking and enjoying spiritual maturity

We are usually in several stages at a time. Very few of us march along from one clear-cut stage to the next. Throughout our lives we are engaging in change and it is scary and unsettling. Reflecting on some of our "passages" can nourish and teach us as our lives unfold.

Our Daily Choices Make a Difference Over Time

All our activities, whether physical, social, spiritual, or psychological, call for daily decisions, some large, some small. We may feel at times that decisions were forced on us because of circumstances and pressures. A young mother, for example, may stay married to an abusive spouse because divorce would put her on welfare—a less tolerable situation to her than struggling in the marriage.

At other times, our decision points are so subtle we hardly realize we have made a choice until hindsight makes it evident. Nancy's mother, Anna, is an example of someone sliding into a way of life unaware of what is happening.

Philosopher Ortega y Gasset, a well-respected thinker and observer of life, spoke at a series of lectures at the University of Madrid in 1932 and 1933 on the subject of choice in time. He took great care to build his argument that to be alive is to continually decide what we are going to be, what our futures are going to be like. At the very root of our lives, Gasset stated, is the time element, because as we are making choices we are deciding our futures.

Many of us seem to be afraid of the future—we want to hold back time, and prevent change. Perhaps we feel that time is our enemy, waiting to destroy us, so we get caught in a frantic need to "save" time by doing everything faster and faster. Questions we may ponder are: What are we saving time for? How do we look at time? Do we accept our power of choice and its ability to mold the future?

We need to learn how to be partners with time, not fight it or control it. In the present moment is our power. Now is the time to be awake to the choices before us—the small, incremental moves that shape our future and set our life course.

Since our days are made up of many small tasks, how we choose to handle them becomes very important. Laura's story is illuminating.

LAURA AND THE GROCERIES

Laura's story and lesson comes out of the most mundane of tasks—buying groceries. In her middle forties, Laura combined family responsibilities with the challenge of a job and often felt harried, stretched to her limit.

On a typical day, running late, Laura rushed to the grocery store on her way home. Grabbing a cart, she yanked several times to get it loose. The grocery aisles beckoned—bright colors, catchy TV jingles sang in her mind, advertised images demanded she take note and buy. Her mind, like a merry-go-round chanted, "What'll I fix?" "What'll they eat?" "What won't take too long?" "What won't cost too much?" "What's healthy?" "Hurry, the kids will be home, hurry!" Laura had come to hate grocery shopping.

She pushed the five-bags-heavy cart out of the store, across a sloppy, puddly, gray parking lot. She lifted the bags into the car, drove home, lifted them out again and carried them to the kitchen counter. Hurry, hurry. How much longer will this take?

Suddenly a blinding awareness slashed through her thoughts. Stop. STOP! This is the only moment you have.

46

Take a breath. Now is all there is! NOW! The quality of your life pivots on this moment. How are you living it?

As Laura breathed deeply, the fuming and complaining began to disappear from her mind. Her body relaxed. She looked more clearly at what she was holding in her hand and ruminated. "Carrots. What excellent works of art they are. So fresh, the green tops still crisp in their lacy goodness. The vibrant tap roots singing with their hallelujah orange. How blessed I am to have plenty to choose from, plenty to eat."

Laura centered herself, gratitude replacing anger. She sensed the sacred in the moment. "Now is the only time I have. The way I choose to live and think right *now* determines the shape of my future. And, beyond that, the thoughts I have now contribute in some small yet powerful way to the future of all—love or fear, harmony or disharmony, peace or war."

With small changes in her attitude such as this one, Laura is making the conscious decision to move toward generativity, and a more rewarding life. She doesn't always manage to do it well, but she rescues herself more quickly now from the old, self-defeating thought patterns. This new path will pay off over time, as Laura consciously cultivates new choices.

Moses and Choice— For Ourselves, for Our Children

This belief in responsibility for the choices and directions of one's life has roots deep in our heritage. The Judeo-Christian scriptures tell the story of Moses and his speech to the people of the fledgling nation, Israel. Moses dramatically set before them the potential for future benefit or

disaster that their choices would bring. He laid out behaviors he believed would lead toward a healthy, positive
future and also warned about choices that could bring negative consequences. At the end he said simply, "I have set
before you life and death, the blessing and the curse. So
choose life in order that you might live, you and your
descendents."

The metaphors of life and death serve to highlight Moses'
belief in the power of the Israelites' choice, both individually and collectively, to shape their future. Not only was *their*
future shaped by their choices, but their descendents' future
as well. Moses realized that succeeding generations would
be affected positively or negatively by today's choices.

Native Americans extend this time of impact to the seventh generation. In their council meetings, when a tribal
issue came before the elders, they weighed the far-reaching
effects of the decision under consideration—how the consequences of the action would affect the seventh generation
yet to come.

We also need to cultivate the skill of farsightedness. How
we choose to live every stage of our lives has far-reaching
outcomes, even to the survival of humankind itself.

Changing Patterns

When we begin to choose consciously and with increased
farsightedness, we do battle with different parts of ourselves.
For example, part of me wants to be loving and patient while
another aspect feels hostile and intolerant. Or, I recognize that
I want to let go and forgive injustices, but that is in conflict
with the part of me that wants to nurse grievances and be
vindictive. Unless I take time to consider the conflicting

demands of these different parts, and make a definite choice, the strongest ones will take over.

One of my strong characteristics is a desire to please, not offend, others. Sometimes this leads me to sabotage myself because I am bending to outer dictates, forsaking my own inner knowing. I wrote the following story after one such experience of giving way to what other people seemed to want of me. This story deals with a large social event. I do not enjoy large events and when I let myself get dragged into one I feel tortured!

RITUALIZED TORTURE

David would be coming home about five o'clock to bathe and dress. We were invited to an elegant party, sponsored by a civic-minded organization, to honor a couple who gave generously of their time and energy. The invitation had requested a hefty charitable donation. Events such as these are often a subject of disagreement between us. However, I had said yes to this one.

I planned to be finished with the bathroom and bedroom at the agreed-upon time so David could have his turn. I knew what I would wear—a creamy, crinkly silk skirt and a simple, soft white top. My antique jade and silver necklace was the perfect complement. I enjoy dressing up sometimes. It is fun to feel elegant.

The Thursday evening party began at six o'clock. We decided to arrive late and avoid a long cocktail hour. The sumptuous hotel entrance was ruled by an imperiously arranged floral tower. Soft swishes from shoes accompanied long stretches of carpet. Finally a baroque sign gaudily proclaimed The Grand Ballroom.

49

The wide, impressive staircase invited the invited to the balcony outside the ballroom. Gaining a party feeling, I anticipated a glass of cool wine with tasty hors d'oeuvres. I hoped to find some compatible people who were eager to have challenging or playful conversation.

The crowd on the balcony clustered shoulder to shoulder in random groupings. There were lines to get the reserved table numbers, lines at the bar, and, later, lines for the bathrooms. About 500 people were expected.

We greeted our soon-to-be-honored friends who were surrounded by well wishers. Everyone was decidedly bright and hearty. Well cared-for teeth gleamed in determined smiles. I looked about for the imagined hors d'oeuvres—they were nowhere to be seen. Then I noticed silver bowls of potato chips. Disdaining the chips, I resigned myself to my hunger.

I noticed that David seemed happily ensconced in conversation and I withdrew from the crowd. I found a vantage point from which to scan the scene. Many of the city's rich and elegant were there, interspersed with concerned, not-for-profit types. A few, like myself, stood alone on the outskirts of things, but hundreds, in cocktail dresses and dark suits, were densely clustered, drinking on empty stomachs. Decibels of noise spiraled higher, responding to tongue-loosening alcohol and crowded conditions.

Eventually the lights dimmed, a sign that dinner was served. The crowd oozed toward the ballroom like some giant, primordial protoplasm, flowing around the corners, fanning out here, pulling in there. Venetian chandeliers hung from Renaissance ceilings and the rosebud-cherub-gilt decor whispered of European

50

courts, sweeping gowns, chivalry, harpsichords, and waltzes.

Musicians churned the space with overwhelming sound waves enhanced by giant speakers. A singer with long, blonde hair and a short, black skirt belted her throat-vibrating all into a seductive microphone. David shouted to me, "Our table's over here."

Black-garbed waiting staff efficiently served the first course, hot bouillon, to half-drugged guests. The musicians played on and the singer sang on. I attempted to speak to the woman seated on my left. Only a few inches separated us, but it was difficult to hear. I strained to catch enough words to guess at what the missing ones probably were. I could feel the veins in my neck protruding as I shouted replies to what I imagined she said.

An interesting man sat on the other side of the woman—an acquaintance of mine for many years. I would have liked to ask him how things were going in his life. I knew his wife was struggling with a long illness. However, it was impossible to be heard over the roar. There seemed to be a deliberate conspiracy to prevent any meaningful communication between the people gathered.

I felt the tiredness of my feet in their unaccustomed high heels. I kicked them off under cover of the tablecloth. I seldom wear heels now, but I had conceded to social norms for this event—only now I was sorry. Social pressure, I mused, the monolith to which I bowed tonight, is a mindless taskmaster.

The award program commenced: speechifying, eulogizing, clapping, and parading tediously devoured the time. By now guests were slipping away; tomorrow

51

was a working day. I too wanted to slip away. When we finally did, I had a stiff body, sore neck, hoarse voice, ringing ears, and a feeling of too much to drink (wine on an empty stomach does not suit me these days).

In the night, I tossed fitfully, pondering the evening. It was a form of torture for me, physically, emotionally, and spiritually—was it for others? I observed many who gushed to one another, "What a lovely party; isn't this fun?" It was not fun for me—am I so different? Maybe it was a bit like the children's story *The Emperor's New Clothes,* in which none of the adults had the courage to trust their perceptions and a giant collusion resulted— broken only by a little child who naively told the truth!

The restless night continued and nourishing sleep eluded me. I knew that first thing in the morning I needed to call and make a date with my chiropractor; my back was out.

I accepted an invitation that I really did not want to accept because I did not have the courage to say no. Lack of courage is becoming increasingly repugnant to me, and I've decided my inability to say no is too costly. I will choose differently next time. There are times in life when we decide to accept invitations or say yes to things that are somewhat unpleasant because we feel they are important. But if we do it because we are not brave enough to choose differently, we can undermine more essential goals—and erode our power to choose and to change.

The Seven Steps of Choice and Change

When considering changes that need to be made, what might the pattern of the choice process look like?

First, you may have a growing uneasiness with what already is. For example, in the story of the Dangerous Ritual, David and I were increasingly uncomfortable with our current situation. The great Indian leader, Gandhi, had this advice to offer those considering change: Never change anything until the thing you want in its place is worth more to you than the thing you are giving up.

Consider these questions once more:

1. What will happen if I continue my old pattern?
2. Is this what I really want for myself?
3. Am I ready to accept the consequences of what I am currently choosing—consequences to both myself and others?
4. What do I *really* want instead?

Second, you gradually become aware that an opportunity for choice is upon you. Like the traveler in Robert Frost's poem, you need to walk the terrain of your life with enough openness and reflection to be able to see the fork in the path ahead. Then you can give yourself the golden opportunity to exercise your power of choice.

Third, you begin to actively check out options that may more adequately meet your long-range goals and desires. Find the home place inside of you where you know what you *really* want—then your choices will be healing for you. They will also be good for others because they will express worthwhile qualities—truth, honor, compassion, forgiveness, health, love, courage, and more.

Fourth, realize there will be some pain and stress involved in giving up your former ways, even if they are destructive. Counting the costs ahead of time will help you to be better prepared. Take an internal checkup, to see if it is appropriate now to take on change and endure a time of instability, stress, or risk as you practice a new attitude or behavior.

Fifth, be aware of some forms of resistance you may use to avoid facing the choice that has come to you. Resistance may include projection, rationalization, anger, or withdrawal. Projection means defending present behavior by blaming circumstances or people. Rationalization means finding reasons to justify the way we are now. Becoming angry and withdrawing—being unwilling to listen—is a way of protecting the status quo. But if we can accept our resistances, let them have their say, we can break their grip on us.

Sixth, gain some sense of how the desired attitudes and behaviors feel, then practice them. It may take forty, fifty, a hundred or more practice times before a new behavior is in place. Laura, for example, is practicing her new behavior of living in the present and being grateful for all parts of her life—even grocery shopping.

Here's an example of my own: I decided that I wanted to drink water instead of other drinks. I had always thought of water as boring, the last thing I would choose to drink for pleasure. That was four years ago. I began my behavior change by tasting the different waters available and I was surprised to find very different flavors. I found spring water that I really enjoyed and experimented with a wedge of lime or a lemon slice in it. Instead of reaching for a different beverage, I began fixing myself a pretty glass of water. I practiced.

Today, water is the first thing I reach for. My body sends out signals when it wants water. I imagine my inner organs glistening with healthy moisture and I feel as if I am giving myself a gift. As a result of my decision to drink water, I have become more finely tuned to my body's needs, and it is a most rewarding change.

Finally, as the new skill becomes more natural we will enjoy a sense of accomplishment and increased self-esteem. The new skill forms part of the foundation upon which other new behaviors and skills can be based. We have successfully created a component in our lives that will bring rewards over the long term.

To summarize, the seven steps contributing to successful choice and change are:

1. Growing discomfort with what is
2. Realization of a need to choose
3. Checking out options
4. Counting the cost
5. Awareness of resistances
6. Practice, practice, practice
7. Enjoying long term rewards

A process such as this could take a long time, depending on how long we linger in the different steps, and how often we repeat the steps—how many games we play with ourselves.

Positive change brings long-term pleasure, but it takes effort. For example, I had long known that I needed a new computer system. My old one was obsolete and I couldn't get parts for it. But since learning a new system is hard, I put it off until it became unavoidable. Here's my poem about that experience:

It could do everything—it promised so much
And besides, my old system had bitten the dust.
It took a big loan and two days in the store
But all that's behind me; ahead—a new door!

The parcels arrived on a cold winter's day
Three loads from the truck—I began to turn gray

A shiver of fear traveled up my old spine
"What on earth have you done?" moaned a part of my
    mind.

Boxes all opened, I surveyed the high tech
Warnings and warranties, there was so much to check!
The computer was light, the directions were not
Software and DOS—I began to feel hot.

I needed instruction to read these instructions
"I must be too stupid," was my dreary deduction.
"Keeping up with these times is too much for me
I should just be irrelevant and watch more TV!"

I called the nice man who sold me this mess
I moaned and complained, a victim of stress
Suicide or murder, both offered release
Tortured, my mind lost all semblance of peace.

In spite of my onslaught and obvious peeve
He retained his professional manner with me
He bolstered my ego (though I felt like an ass)
And my future turned round with his words:
"Take a class!"

If we persevere with change, we will build confidence in ourselves. By the way—I love my new computer system and now wonder why I waited so long!

Accepting What We Can't Change
Changes Everything! Marcia's Mystery

A realistic and courageous assessment of our lives will reveal that we can change and influence some things, but other situations we must learn to accept. Some conditions cannot be changed—we need to have food, shelter, pay

56

taxes, and so on. Certain situations and people somehow appear in our lives—even though we didn't necessarily plan it that way.

How we react to these happenings is vital to our well-being. In my own life I realized that if David and I were to be married, we had to fully accept each other's children—creative acceptance was called for. I had thought my parenting responsibilities were over and now I had a thirteen-year-old step-daughter who would be living with us. The creative acceptance that I speak of takes time and often goes through several stages. Acceptance of a situation that we cannot change, paradoxically can change everything. Marcia's story will illustrate this paradox.

Edward could hardly face the reality of what had come into his life. His beloved wife, Marcia, had cancer, and he couldn't understand the meaning of it all. They had lived their lives honestly, trying to do the best they could, raising two children, working hard. He couldn't understand a God of love allowing such suffering as Marcia (and all of them) endured.

It made matters worse that everyone was concerned for them. "I know the best treatment, fly to Mexico and. . . ." "In Dallas there is a faith healer, I sent him your name. . . ." "Mommie, why doesn't God make you well?" "If you only believed, Marcia, God would heal you." "Marcia, what negative thoughts have you been holding on to? Just release them and you will find positive healing energies coming into you." It was all so confusing. He knew she had tried it all.

Marcia pondered her life. Where had she gone wrong? What if she could believe, really believe? She did feel a Presence around her at times. She knew she was loved and connected to much more than could be explained with her mind.

As Easter approached, the family made preparations with a heavy heart. "Daddy, will we color eggs this year?" "Will we go to the big church breakfast after the sun comes up and Jesus is not dead anymore?" "Can Mommie go?"

Within Marcia's heart—a Gethsemane. "Oh God, please let me recover. I have children to raise. It is not my time, I know it in my heart. I am even grateful for this disease when I consider what I have learned, the perspective I have gained." Here, Marcia would move beyond words into the timeless void, where the everlasting arms could sometimes be felt.

Easter morning the family dressed and left for their sunrise service. With Edward's help, Marcia sat at a place on the beach where their church members liked to gather for the early Easter celebrations. The dawn was pink, gold, and purple, the air crisp and sea-washed. Children were running about in excitement, people talked in little groups. The celebration of the resurrection was beginning.

In that place where earth, water, darkness, and light meet, Marcia's spirit hovered. She made a vow deep within herself, a vow that changed her relationship with everything. "God, whoever and wherever you are, if you spare my life, it is yours, but I surrender, Lord. I surrender into what is, whatever that is, death or life."

A deep sigh began in the base of Marcia's spine and made its way up through her whole body. Marcia's awareness was so heightened she could feel a tingle at the level of her cells. All else was blotted out. It was a holy moment, a moment when heaven and earth were one. The moment gradually receded like a gentle but powerful wave.

The little family returned home after the celebrations. Marcia's new acceptance and peace made itself felt in the everydayness of their lives. Marcia saw with her newly opened spiritual eyes a need for an understanding community to surround those who suffered as she was suffering with the dreaded cancer. People are so afraid of cancer that they want to blame the sufferer for bringing it on themselves. She no longer judged people who accused her of having little faith, but in her growing joy and forgiveness, she had compassion for them.

Acceptance, a Generative Move

Marcia's deep experience of finally surrendering into what she could not change brought her a peace that was not dependent on the course of her disease. When she was able to let go of trying to control the uncontrollable, her family benefitted. The children relaxed, not needing to respond to Marcia's tension. Marcia's church began a support group for people who were ill, and also formed groups for their families. Marcia could see that her experience was helping others and it made her feel useful, productive.

In Native American wisdom, wholeness is seen as the fullness with which one stays in the moment, not the length of one's life. With her new spirit of acceptance, Marcia entered into a time of living fully each moment that came to her. She spoke with renewed love to her children. She was truthful with them—but also reassuring. The children knew that they could depend on their mother to tell the truth, so they believed her when she said they would be all right. Marcia creatively accepted her illness, and thought of ways to bless her children in the years ahead. She wrote them letters, entrusted to her husband, one letter for each growing-up year to be opened on their birthdays.

Marcia perceived herself as living in her body-home temporarily, leasing it for a time. In the year she had left, Marcia began to live, really live the process of her dying. Her faith was strengthened and she knew her spirit would go on. When Marcia completed her life, the room was filled with a feeling of love and gentle peace as she quietly slipped out of her body.

CHAPTER FOUR

Lives To Learn From

The Child is father of the Man.

—WILLIAM WORDSWORTH

THE DAY WHEN I FINALLY faced that I was half a century old and the river of my life was moving steadily onward to its mysterious destination was a major transition and an incredible gift. Facing my mortality was a crisis because I began to recognize some very painful fears about getting old—fears that eventually turned into guides for my life. I tell this story here hoping that it will encourage those of you who are concerned about making changes and worried about the cost involved, financial and otherwise.

Out of my time of facing the inevitability of growing older emerged my resolve to learn more about positive aging. I wanted to meet and talk with people in the second half of their lives who had the respect of others in their communities. My need to find and learn from people who seemed to be aging in positive ways became an inner resource for me.

My desire to go back to school came in my middle forties. My marriage was ending and I could see I would be entering a new era in my life. My former husband was opposed to my returning to school, but I knew I had to. It was an inner imperative. Although I had worked off and on all my adult life, my career track was rather like a patchwork quilt and I didn't feel I would have a rewarding or financially secure future without a college degree.

I had an image of a terrible job for an older woman like myself: selling ladies' hosiery at our local department store. Often when I went there to pick up this or that I saw weary, footsore, older women who stood all day, day after day. I had developed a motivating terror that that might eventually happen to me.

I completed college and pursued a master's degree, but I still felt unsettled. Taking some time off at a simple retreat center in the Arizona desert, I reflected on my life and where I was going. It was an important time, living in a simple room with the whole desert outside my door. I experienced solitude and silence. Several important insights came from that time—one was the importance of following my deepest desires.

I moved to a university town about seventy-five miles away from home and began doctoral studies. I was scared. It was a big step for me, at age forty-eight, to quit my job and move. Money was scarce and I had two almost-grown children who still needed some financial support.

I invested in a run-down house with suitable space to rent to students and began fixing it up. I also got a job at the university. Although it barely paid minimum wage, the perks were good. And I will be forever grateful for the student loans that helped me at this time.

Even though I worked very hard, I had lots of help along the way, wonderful "coincidences" that encouraged and aided me. One person particularly comes to mind. I kept hearing of a new professor who was coming to the university, a recognized scholar in adult education and development. Then I found out that I had just moved across the street from her!

Sharan Merriam and I became friends. Both of us were divorced, single parents, and new to both the community and the university. We enjoyed each other from the beginning. She became a mentor for me, guiding my studies and sharing herself in a generous way. (You, too, will be surprised by help from unexpected quarters as you step out to make needed changes.) I loved my studies and found them to be in harmony with what I wanted to learn. But sometimes I struggled with feelings of guilt and selfishness because I had left friends and family to pursue my goals.

Lives to Learn From

In the next few chapters, I will tell you about some people age forty to seventy-seven who are highly generative, people who found their purpose in life and were committed to understanding themselves and learning to care in healthier ways for both themselves and others. I found their stories vital and unique, even though themes of commonality wove them into a cohesive pattern.

Generativity, successful aging, for them, did not suddenly arrive in the middle years. It was built on roots or themes that came from childhood. Because *caring* is the main quality associated with generativity, I decided to trace the elements of caring they received in childhood.

The concept of caring includes the idea of protection, attention, providing for, affection for. Love can sometimes be used interchangeably, but when we speak of love, often we are thinking in terms of an intimate relationship that we hold dear. Both love and caring are vital to all of us, but the larger, less exclusive implications of caring help us understand the concept of generativity better.

The people I interviewed started life with widely varying backgrounds, resources, handicaps, and opportunities. Some were born with all the advantages; others struggled with poverty, coming out of the Depression or from a low-income group. Some had no formal education after high school, but as adults returned for further study. Others studied only a short time at college, and still others earned multiple degrees at some of the most elite universities in the country.

Some bore the burdens of racism and prejudice; others had early physical limitations like blindness or hearing impairment. One was an only child; another came from a family of twelve. Although the early childhood worlds of these people varied enormously, they shared three themes in common: they could identify the sources of caring in their childhood, they observed how people cared for others, and they developed a capacity for empathy as a result of their own hardships. Perhaps you can see some of yourself and your background in one of these stories.

Sources of Caring in Childhood

Every person in this group could recall experiences of being loved and cared for by someone in childhood, but the degrees and sources for this caring varied widely. Most

64

sought and received caring from people outside their immediate families as well—grandparents, other relatives, and teachers.

In general, the backgrounds of these people fell into three categories: those who experienced a great deal of caring in their families of origin, those who received some caring at home but felt that the love and acceptance was conditional, and those who were mainly rejected and isolated from parents.

The first type of home environment, a very caring family, appeared in Roberta's story. I drove to her neighborhood in Chicago's south side, following her instructions carefully. The housing projects looked dreary, forbidding, even sinister. I came to her street of row houses, and one stood out. It had tulips blooming in the tiny fenced-in yard. Patches of grass struggled to grow in the hard earth. Roberta answered the door. A fairly large woman in her middle sixties with her gray hair neatly pulled back, she had an air of quiet strength about her.

The living room was lively with bright colors. I could tell that Roberta used her house for classes—for construction paper art was widely displayed, giving the place a youthful, schoolroom feeling. I saw large sacks of produce and other essential foodstuffs stacked in corners. Roberta's compassionate actions on behalf of the people in her neighborhood were the reason I was interviewing her. We sat at a table together and she shared her story—one that begins here and will unfold more fully later on.

Roberta was born into a black family, one of twelve children. Her twin died in infancy. She has lived all her life on one street, which today borders some housing projects. In looking back on her childhood, she recalled:

> I had a father I could be proud of even though he was
> only a common laborer. He could sing; he was very
> talented. My parents were together fifty-four years; they
> were strong and loving people.
>
> They gave us good lessons. They weren't able to edu-
> cate us as far as a college education. My mother took in
> laundry to supplement what Dad could do. We knew we
> were loved. We were punished when we did wrong, but
> somehow you got the message—you are loved.

Another story of childhood beginnings came from Peter.
The stories of Peter and Roberta seem, at first blush, to have
little in common. Peter is an international figure, wealthy,
and Jewish. He lives on Chicago's Gold Coast. Underneath
the surface differences, however, Roberta and Peter share
an unshakable bond that transcends social and cultural influences. They are creative, thoughtful, giving, vital people
who, in their sixties and seventies, model the qualities of
generativity that are so inspiring.

At age seventy-seven, Peter looks forward with enthusiasm to each day. Lean and attractive, Peter exudes vitality.
We met in his handsome high-rise offices.

Peter was born in the early 1900s of newly immigrated
parents. He was reared in a kosher, Yiddish-speaking home
in the Midwest. Peter's father earned a modest living making shoes; his mother was overly indulgent. Peter described
himself and his family:

> I was a chubby kid; if I didn't eat more, my mother
> would suffer. . . . I liked to read and eat. I was a teacher's
> pet. I came from a family that cared—in their religion,
> in their contributions, modest though they were, taking
> people in who didn't have anything. It's a tradition of

66

our people that you take care of those who are less well-off. Their example lived on with me.

Peter and Roberta both felt the underlying love and attentive concern that was available for them in their childhood homes. However, other childhood difficulties came their way later.

Two more people, Barbara and Elloah, also spoke of homes where they were validated and felt deeply cared for. Barbara, however, struggled with a major handicap.

I rang the doorbell of Barbara's tidy little white house situated close to a train station and heard a dog bark in response. The door opened, and with a radiant smile that balanced her blank eyes, Barbara greeted me. She was a slim, energetic-appearing woman in her middle sixties with dark hair mixed with a little gray. She asked me immediately if I minded dogs. I assured her that I didn't. Barbara is blind, and her affection for her Seeing Eye dog was obvious. "She is such a dear friend," she explained simply. The dog lay by Barbara's feet as we began our time together.

Barbara spoke of growing up in the comfort of a large, caring family where there was always something going on. She was blinded at age three in an accident. The incident deeply affected her whole family, but Barbara never doubted for a moment that she was deeply loved. She spoke of her mother:

> Mother had a positive approach to all things and an absolute faith that was strong, but it must have been put to the test when she was faced with bringing me up as a totally blind child. Mother never allowed me to feel sorry for myself. My parents provided a lot of stimulation for me—horseback riding, swimming.

Today, Barbara, a grandmother, delights in her eight grand-children and babysits them regularly. Word has spread through that young group that although Grandma can't see them, she hears everything! But, as you will see later in Barbara's story, she knows herself to be much more than a grandmother, as important as that is to her.

I felt privileged to have found the generous-spirited Bar-bara. A major difficulty like being blind could turn a person sour. It certainly is one of my fears—to lose my eyesight. So when I heard of Barbara and her radiant, courageous ap-proach to life in spite of its inequities, I wanted to know her and learn from her.

Elloah was the only person I interviewed who was born outside the United States. I envy the benefits of her large, intergenerational family. We in the States have lost so many of those benefits.

It was a rainy Sunday afternoon when Elloah and I met. She works at a nursing home and we met at the end of her shift. She has an engaging smile that flashes easily, lighting up the space around her. Her black eyes dance, especially as she begins to talk of her childhood. She described her caring home in the West Indies. She explained that in her native culture each child was really the responsibility of the entire town. Everyone knew each other and children were a wel-come asset to all.

I pressed her for specific memories of her parents. "My mother was a caring person. She was always giving, encour-aging other people, especially young people, and I find myself doing the same thing." Her encouraging and giving attitudes in her sometimes-difficult job had won the respect of people in her community, and she had been interviewed on a lo-cal television program. Elloah sings to her sick, dependent, and sometimes-crotchety patients as she goes about her daily chores.

The stories of Roberta, Peter, Barbara, and Elloah began to teach me that people could be enjoying the rewards of generativity whether their scope of caring was small or large, whether they were rich or poor. It seemed to be more an attitude, a response to life that nurtured and enriched their activities.

Let's look now at some people who remembered some very different childhood experiences. Several felt there had been a mixture of both caring and hurtful behaviors in their childhood homes. They experienced caring but it was compromised by other dynamics. One woman from this second category of home environment represented this viewpoint:

> I think the prevailing thing in my family was having to look right. A lot of energy went into the image of the family and how that looked to the outside world. Although I have to say, my parents were also caring people.

Many of us can identify with this kind of value in our childhoods. It was certainly true in my own childhood home. "What will the neighbors think?" was a phrase I grew up with. I remember being exhorted to wash between my toes and behind my ears—not because being clean felt so good, but in case I was in an accident the doctor might see the dirt.

The people in my study who didn't receive healthy caring and instead felt rejected and isolated by parents fit into the third category of home environment. For them, home could be a frightening, dangerous place. These people spoke of childhood suffering and seeking support outside their homes.

69

One man whose parents were uncaring stated: "I hated my dad. He was too busy. He just didn't have time for us." Two women particularly remember their mothers: "I've had to keep my distance from a very controlling mother." "As a young child I was very withdrawn. I had a rather dangerous mother. She had no boundaries. I was daddy's girl and mother was jealous."

Home environments of this type often leave children anxious, lonely, unable to feel close to others. Absentee fathers are often neglectful without even being aware of it. Too much control from parents is punitive, and a jealous parent is often given to rages, accusations, and threats, weakening a young child's sense of self-esteem and value.

When parents have boundary problems, they are busy minding another's business; they are invasive and the children do not feel safe. For example, such parents may open the door to their children's rooms without knocking, or perhaps eat off their plates without asking or read their teen's diary. Children of these types of parents feel pressured to be good and to please the parents, with the result that they sacrifice their real selves. They are unable to develop their own separate individuality. Instead, they usually form false-self systems while trying to please their parents and be safe.

Lewis, the last person in this category, struggled just to survive in childhood. I had first met him about ten years earlier when a group of my friends and I audited a course he taught at a leading university. He was a man of understanding and compassion, qualities all his students appreciated. He sometimes found himself in hot water with the conservative elements in his university because he wanted to introduce innovative and student-centered teaching practices.

Lewis began life in a wealthy but destructive environment. His difficulties were compounded by some birth

70

defects, which made him an embarrassment to his parents. They mistakenly thought him feeble minded. They attempted to hide him and refused to let him eat with the family because his handicaps made him messy at the table. Lewis described his early childhood as terrible, living in the "chaos of rejection, turned over to maids." He was able to overcome or compensate for his handicaps to a large extent in later life, but he remembered with lingering emotion the destructiveness in his home and how its impact often made him physically sick as a child:

> The lack of love in our house could have destroyed
> me. It was really evil. I was dealing as a child with the
> evil of rejection. It was just a struggle to survive. Many
> people are destroyed by rejection like this. One of my
> goals is to try to do something about that!

Beyond the home and immediate family most of the women and men in emotionally deprived homes turned to caring grandparents, other relatives, or teachers for support, understanding, and encouragement. Those who found caring from grandparents spoke warmly about them. The man whose father was always too busy to spend time with him spoke of his grandfather: "I had a grandpa who was one of the greatest. He gave me the sense of being a kid and of the joy of life!"

The two women who had difficult mothers were successful in receiving love from their grandmothers. One remembered:

> My grandmother prayed for me. It meant a lot to
> know that. She would send us things, like at Easter a
> box with a cake in it that she baked. I would always

think it was so tender of her—to bake a cake. I get teary remembering that.

Teachers can be wonderful caregivers, a resource for children. I hope those of you who are teachers or who are involved in any way with children will find encouragement in these stories. Those who work with children often wonder if all the effort and commitment is worth it. Many who experienced caring from teachers expressed gratitude for the continuing gifts of those early influences.

Roberta, from the ghetto environment of Chicago's south side, sometimes didn't have appropriate school clothes, so her mother would keep her home from school. One day Roberta needed shoes before she could go to school, but there were none in the house that fit her. Her father's paycheck was due in a few days and her mother promised the shoes then.

A sensitive and compassionate teacher noticed Roberta's absence and called at her home to see what the problem was. After appraising the situation, she invited the little girl to come to a special room at school, carefully instructing her to go through a side door where she could not be seen. The teacher knew well the thoughtless cruelty of school children toward someone who has a problem.

Roberta discovered a miracle room the teacher called her "wardrobe room." It was filled with clothing all neatly mended, cleaned, and ready to wear. When a needy child came to her attention, the teacher and the child would select the needed items, and the child would leave school unobserved carrying a plain brown bag. Roberta learned much from that experience.

Lewis, the loved and respected professor, also received a much-needed boost from a teacher. Now in his late sixties,

Lewis spoke of being brain damaged and hearing impaired at birth. This condition brought him many hardships. To-day, however, he is a noted author with twenty-three books in print. In spite of a slight speech impediment, he lectures all over the world. But it has been a long journey from an ignored and hurting child to a successful, older scholar.

The first real hope came to Lewis in fifth grade. There he found a wonderful teacher "who saw I had potential and gave me courage." Maybe this early influence is one of the reasons why Lewis's classes are so sought after. He recognizes the potential in his students and gives them courage—there could be no finer gift.

Peter's experience of a caring teacher came in a different form, with harsh words from a college teacher. True caring will always dare to name the truth in a creative and loving way when the time is right. When we care, we are not engaged in a popularity contest.

At home Peter had been caught in a dilemma. He had a mother who "would suffer if I didn't eat more." So, Peter ate. When he arrived at the university, he carried 212 pounds on his five-foot six-inch frame. Peter's physical-education teacher took one look at him and gave him living hell. The confrontation went like this: "Young man, you are destroying your life!" The teacher was tough, Peter remembered, but "I lost sixty-five pounds in six months and he started me on a routine, part of which I maintain to this day." The teacher remained a friend for life.

Most of us can identify with one of the three types of home environments we've discussed. Perhaps we found most of our caring in our original families, or we remember our home as one where we received a combination of caring and difficulty, or perhaps we found mainly rejection from parents and sought caring outside our homes with varying degrees of success. The last is the type of home I grew up in. My grandmother and the love I felt from her pulled me through my childhood.

How we responded to our childhood experiences contributes to who we are today. Most of us need to do some work to reclaim the good parts of our childhood experiences while gaining perspective and finding freedom from the destructive and damaging elements. The popularity of John Bradshaw's writings and television sessions on healing the inner child bears witness to this need. Bradshaw and others are helping many of us gain the insights and skills necessary to become whole as adults, reconnecting with that part of us left behind in childhood. Our adulthood will not be free if our inner child is still imprisoned.

Children Watch How People Care for Others

The people I interviewed recalled how they watched those around them demonstrate caring for others. The many ways they observed people treating others turned out to be key experiences.

Several people in the group learned about caring by observing uncaring behaviors. They were angered when they saw a lack of basic respect for others. They observed judgments, elitism, and prejudice in the way people interacted with "outsiders." Even as children they vowed to behave differently.

Elloah, born in the West Indies where many nationalities live together, remembered how families showed tolerance for differences and respect for all people. When she came to the United States and began to raise her darker-skinned children here, she was shocked at the discrimination they experienced.

Churches and synagogues provided good resources for caring that reached beyond the confines of the family. Peter spoke of early memories. As a little boy he would drop coins into a special container at his synagogue to help finance the dream of a Jewish homeland across the ocean. His family also took people into their home who were in special need, sharing their resources for a time.

Peter learned another lesson—how it felt to be discriminated against. He was a member of the Hi-Y Club, which he enjoyed very much. When it came time to elect a new president and Peter had all the qualifications, he was told that a Jew couldn't become president.

Another member of the group, a dentist, who has donated his skills for extended periods of time in needy areas all over the world, remembered his experiences in the armed forces. There he saw blatant racial prejudice for the first time:

> I'd never run into that when I was a boy, but when
> I got into the service and heard some of the Texas boys
> talk to some of the blacks that came into the clinic,
> I couldn't believe my ears! You know, you're just
> not accustomed to talking to another human being
> that way!

Childhood Difficulties Fostered Empathy

In childhood and adolescence all the people in the group experienced difficulties—difficulties that could have warped them or made them hostile. Yet, this did not happen over the long term. The very adversities that hurt them instead encouraged them to develop a compassion that grew— eventually turning into the quality of personality we call generativity. Their difficult experiences cultivated their ability to identify with and have empathy for others. Empathy is the ability to have the power to project yourself into another's life and comprehend what it means to be that person. This compassionate quality, which began in childhood and continued into adulthood, was an important component in helping these people to age successfully.

Creative transformation like this is a mysterious process. One wonders how some people use difficulties to learn and grow, transcending ugliness and pain to gain pleasure from giving, while others end up distorted or disheartened from deprivations and hardships. How can we learn to turn liabilities into assets? These women and men—without exception—saw their earlier hardships as devices that softened their hearts and helped them to feel and understand another's experience.

CHAPTER FIVE

Entry into Midlife

Wholly unprepared, they embark upon the second half of life. Or are there perhaps colleges for forty-year olds which prepare them for their coming life and its demands as the ordinary colleges introduce our young people to a knowledge of the world and of life? No, there are none. Thoroughly unprepared we take the step into the afternoon of life; worse still, we take this step with the false presupposition that our truths and ideals will serve as hitherto. But we cannot live the afternoon of life according to the programme of life's morning—for what was great in the morning will be little at evening, and what in the morning was true will at evening have become a lie.

—Carl Jung

Carl Jung pointed out how much we need preparation as we go through the midlife transition. I didn't understand much of what was happening to me in my late thirties and forties. Often I felt I was crazy for having some of my reactions and feelings and I was afraid I was the only one who was experiencing those turbulences. Many of you may be in the same boat, wondering what is happening in you and why.

My hope is that as you get a glimpse into the lives of some people who are negotiating the second half of life you will be encouraged as you move through some similar transitions. Sometimes when people make an appointment with me to discuss their midlife concerns, they find that all they really need is some assurance that they are not crazy, and that they are on the right path. With perseverance and a little help from others they will come out on the other side with great strengths and gifts, as the people in my study did.

Roberta, Peter, Barbara, Elloah, and Lewis evolved from their childhood influences into adult life. Now we will look at what they and others considered to be their major life turning points—events and experiences that shook them. Some turning points or pivotal events are dramatic, like the death of a loved one, illness, divorce, or depression, and they result in radical changes in lifestyle. Other turning points are more subtle and result in changes in attitudes and behaviors over time. For example, the challenges of growing children, deep spiritual experiences—and even birthdays.

When the study people spoke of their main pivotal experiences, most saw their middle thirties through early fifties as the time when an essential shift occurred. Sometimes they did not quite realize the impact of certain experiences until later. These men and women found that they took from several years to a decade or more to negotiate a major turning point. From the first invasive happening or upheaval to the completion of that particular event could take more than ten years, but it never took less than several years.

As I studied the important transitional times of each individual, I began to notice three components that everyone shared: a pivotal event or events that necessitated key decisions, a sense of calling that continued to be compelling, and an awareness of the risks and consequences of generative decisions.

Liana's Near-Death Began Her Transition

I met Liana through a mutual acquaintance and quickly respected her talents as a healer and counselor, seeking her services for myself and recommending her to friends. I knew she had experienced a dramatic change in her life about ten years earlier, but until I asked her if I could interview her for this study, I did not know any details.

An attractive, fine-boned woman with classic Mediterranean features framed by a cloud of dark hair, Liana can appear starkly sophisticated or soft and casual. One would never guess she has passed her fiftieth birthday. An artist, Liana was in her early forties when her pivotal experience came. One night she and her husband were entertaining people interested in furthering her art career. She was in the kitchen making last-minute preparations.

Suddenly she felt ill, shaky. She looked at her hands holding a tray of food. They seemed to be turning purple, the color of eggplant skin. With ebbing consciousness she went to the living room and whispered to her husband, "Something's very wrong with me."

He rushed her to the hospital emergency ward. During what appeared to be a blackout, Liana described an ineffable trip through space, seeing vignettes of her life, like pieces of a puzzle, all coming together. She experienced an overwhelming sense of the joy and meaning of life. What appeared to be food poisoning, medically speaking, became a turning point in her life, for Liana returned home a few days later, and nothing seemed the same.

Dramatically affected by her near-death experience, Liana observed, "That event was given to me, I feel, to turn my life around and spiritualize my life."

Entering a time of searching, she looked for teachers to help her make sense of what was happening to her. She attended workshops, read books, and began some therapy. For several years Liana devoted much time to reflecting on her life, sorting out the parts—which to keep, which let go. She changed from the agnosticism of her Jewish family background to a new spirituality, and gradually her career focus changed to reflect some of her new values. Relationships changed as people who could not understand the changes in her drifted away, but people who shared her new values entered her life.

As Liana's entry into her midlife transition came to fruition, she accepted the invitation to become more than what she had been in the first half of her life.

George's Daughter Pushed Him Further

Often our children compel us to grow up. They are an accurate mirror in which to see parts of ourselves and they shake us out of complacency, out of our ruts. This was George's experience.

I first met George the day of our interview. We had agreed to meet at his home, a modest brick structure on a street with big trees. I entered the living room and was immediately drawn to the interesting and unique furnishings from around the world.

George, a dentist, was in his mid-sixties. He was friendly, with thinning hair and glasses. Earlier in his life, he and his wife had spoken vaguely about traveling overseas to a clinic where George could volunteer his dental skills for a brief time. But they had never gotten around to it—that is, until their daughter's plans moved things along.

A college student, she wanted to take a vacation trip of which her parents disapproved. As George and his wife tried to figure out ways to divert her attention from this plan, the idea of a medical tour to a Third World clinic came back into his mind. He and his wife decided on the trip, and asked their daughter to accompany them; she accepted.

George spoke of his surprise the first time he saw a Third World clinic—so different from what he was used to. The conditions under which he was expected to work were primitive. There were no dental chairs—the patient sat in a regular chair while helpers held the patient's head as George worked on the patient's teeth. George's respect for his daughter grew as he saw her pitch in, forgetting herself in her commitment to help: "I was so impressed with the way she worked—it brings tears to my eyes. She was patting heads, holding hands, blood everywhere. . . . "

Because of the challenge George's daughter brought to him, he was, in his words, "backed into giving to others, but I tell you, it was the most thrilling experience of my life!" It was also the beginning of many trips and many years of donating his time, money, and expertise to needy people at clinics abroad.

The Death of His Son Brought Questions

Here we take up Peter's life again. Peter was on the fast track, gaining influence, money, and power. He married and became a father. His life was moving along in an orderly manner toward the culturally accepted goals of "success." Then an event invaded his life, a very painful event. Death took Peter's three-year-old son just six months before a vaccine which would have saved his life was discovered. "He just burned up with fever," remembered this father.

Grief-stricken, and overcome by the loss that triggered so many questions and challenged so many assumptions about life, Peter took a year off from his successful business. He, his wife, and the remaining children traveled to get away from their burden, trying to make sense of their loss. Peter summed up his painful experience: "You don't forget these things; they either destroy or build."

Peter feels that one learns by pain and by experience. Because of his experience, he learned to value life differently, to make the most of it. He learned that he could not control everything, and that life is temporary.

Returning to his home and life, he found his old securities shifting and new values emerging. Very gradually he initiated changes that increasingly reflected these shifts. In the beginning, Peter couldn't have looked into the future to see that he would eventually become an international mediator. We can never predict the long range results of our present choices. If we follow our inner nudges, however, we will be surprised by our interesting and unforseen future.

"Let Me Finish Raising My Children"

Taking another look into Roberta's life, we see her in her early forties, married to a postal worker and the mother of six children. She is in crisis—her life pattern invaded by illness.

Roberta began to experience severe headaches and double vision. At first she tried to ignore it, but on Ash Wednesday in 1966 she collapsed and was hospitalized. Doctors discovered several brain tumors and scheduled surgery for the removal of the tumors and the pituitary gland.

Roberta's five sons and one daughter were teenagers. Gang activity was rampant in their ghetto neighborhood, and Roberta was scared, and worried for her children. The night before her delicate and risky surgery, her anxiety forced her to do some serious thinking about life's meaning. Before dawn she reached a decision and prayed to God fervently, with a whole new intention: "Let me live to finish raising my children." She made a promise in her extremity: If she could live, she would serve others the rest of her life.

Roberta not only lived, but her pituitary gland amazingly regenerated itself. As a result, Roberta's outlook underwent a major change—"It was no longer the big 'I,'" she told me. "I became God-centered."

Shortly thereafter, a person came into Roberta's life who would become an enduring influence. A nun, with a vision of how things could be different in Roberta's ghetto neighborhood, became her friend, mentor, prayer partner, and team worker. Together they planned strategies that would meet some of the needs of the poorest of the poor. Through the years, Roberta never forgot her vow.

Sense of Calling

All the men and women interviewed spoke of being called to new directions in their lives. This sense of being called was like finding a life mission and was dramatic for some, more subtle for others. A few may not even be comfortable with that phrase "being called," yet, as the observer, I see something like that happening.

For some the sense of being called was like an inner voice they felt compelled to respond to. For others it was simply a growing certainty. However the sense of call evidenced itself, they all felt compelled to answer yes and to keep answering yes as one change led to another.

What I mean by a sense of call is the process of discovering what you want to do that represents the essential core of who you are. It emerges from within and gives direction and purpose to life. The idea of a life purpose or mission can be an over-arching principle, a unifying theme to which the other aspects of your life, such as job, recreation, relationships, and spiritual path, needs to harmonize.

For example, Dr. Martin Luther King, Jr., gave many speeches in which he expressed his calling, his passion. His desire was that the different races in the United States live and pray together in peace. Everything he did related to this calling. It takes time and perseverance to uncover this kind of deeply held aspiration and life purpose.

Bill's Call

I scheduled my interview with Bill when he was in Chicago for a board meeting. Bill was a handsome man in his late sixties, one of those with a full head of hair. Lean, with a friendly smile, Bill had thought through what he wanted to say. He seemed as interested in telling his story as I was in hearing it.

"I want to lay the groundwork so you'll understand what happened to me," he began carefully. "I was a Depression kid and that made a tremendous impression on me." Bill never remembered being hungry, but he came awfully close to it. A symbol for Bill of the financial problems in his home was the lack of warm winter clothing. Out of that embarrassing and uncomfortable lack he determined that he was going to "make it!"

Other influences formed Bill's value system. When he was ten he began going to church, and had a spiritual experience he still remembers. Working hard came easily. When Bill got his first job at seventy-five dollars a month, the first thing he did was to buy a warm overcoat.

Marriage to his wife, Helen, and becoming the father of three children enriched Bill's life. He kept rising up the corporate ladder until at age forty-five he was vice president of marketing with an international firm. One day Bill's boss asked him to take the job of running the overseas operation. He learned much in those travels, most of which were in the Third World. Some of what Bill experienced was painful. He recalled:

> I had never seen poverty like that. My company did business in ninety-two countries—I saw them all! Confronted with that kind of impact time after time, it begins to do something to you. You don't know where to start, you don't know what to do. I mean you can go down the street and hand out dollar bills but that's no solution. It became a deep frustration to me—seeing hungry kids in doorways.

Then the big break came. A multinational family-owned company offered him the presidency. It was all a Depression kid could have dreamed of and more. Bill and his family built their dream house on a New Jersey hillside. But then some things happened that changed the course of Bill's life.

> I came home one night and Helen said to me, "You know, I have the feeling we're not going to live in this house for very long." I thought she had gone a little— you know. Then I came home another night and I was telling her we just got the latest sales figures and they were way up. She looked at me and said, "Is that what you want to do with your life?" I said, "What do you mean?" She said, "Make rich people richer." I didn't know how to handle that! Gee, here I am—everything is going well, and she asks a question like that.

85

And though this was not a comment Bill particularly wanted to hear, it was true. His efforts and expertise were making the family who owned the company more and more wealthy. Helen's question rankled.

One day Bill and Helen attended a church service where the guest speaker told of the need for small business loans to help enterprising people in the Third World. Bill was animated: "He got only halfway through that idea and I knew clearly that I had to be involved in it! That was my answer! I had to say yes! It was not emotional, but I just knew."

The idea of starting a loan fund for small businesses in Third World countries did not take off easily. Bill went to Washington for funding and was often frustrated by the negative attitudes of people in government agencies. At times he really wanted to tell them to forget it. But something would always happen to keep him from giving up. He explained it this way: "Somehow, God would bring to my mind the faces of those people we were trying to serve." That kept him going.

Twenty years later, in 1991, the organization Bill founded helped enough small businesses get started to provide 12,000 new jobs in various Third World countries.

The last time Bill and Helen were in the Philippines visiting some loan recipients, they were introduced to a young man with quite a story. He had been a drinker, a wife-beater, always in trouble. A fisherman by trade, he was not doing very well. One day he stumbled into a local church and was impressed by some people who lived by very different values. He received some caring attention and heard about possible loans he might be eligible for.

He was voted to receive an $800 loan to buy a boat. He and the three men he hired to help him catch fish became successful at their work, and began distributing extra fish to needy people in the community. He was asked to tell his story to some visiting Americans. Bill told me:

> Now, I didn't understand a word he was saying, but the glow on his face was radiant—we're standing by the boat there on the sand and he was talking and the tears were going down my face. I didn't have to hear what he was saying, I saw the expression on his face. That's the reward! I don't need anything more than that!

A subtle theme in this story is Helen's part. It was Helen's remark "Is that what you want to do with your life—make rich people richer?" that invaded Bill's consciousness and made him increasingly uncomfortable with things as they were. She also supported Bill in his major life changes. I wonder, could he have done this without her influence and support?

Others Experience Their Mission

Roberta's mission was to her own people in their great need. Together with the nun who showed her a new way of living and serving, they developed a workable response to the devastating poverty around them. Over time, Roberta's commitment to her people increased until, after the children had gone and her husband had died, Roberta transformed her row house into a food pantry, clothing wardrobe room, and donated furniture center. She and her coworkers had one goal: to be a resource for the housing development across the street. Today they have workshops on health, money management, housekeeping, and childcare skills. Roberta finds many of her resources through networking with five wealthy white suburban churches to bring goods and services to her neighborhood.

Over the years, Peter, now a multimillionaire, gradually changed his business, recreational, and social priorities to make room for his increasing political and philanthropic endeavors. He has served many United States presidents as well as other world leaders. He feels called to be a conciliator and has worked hard to bring the Palestinians and the Jews into dialogue over their shared land. Peter's mission developed over time, but today it is very clear. "You have to commit yourself to something if you have any sense of honor at all. I believe that there's a purpose in life in making sure others live, too. I can't enjoy life if people are starving."

Other group members said about their decisions and choices, "It's chosen me; I almost feel as though I have no alternative!" Another expressed it this way: "We are called to make the world better. I want to be part of that process."

For these women and men, the tasks and activities to which they felt called reflected who they were at a very deep level. Their new activities made use of the experiences, resources, and abilities they already had even as they developed new strengths.

Through their compassionate actions, these people grew in their ability to make positive contributions. One thing led to another; one choice spawned others, way led on to way.

CHAPTER SIX

Risks and Consequences

In human beings courage is necessary to make being and becoming possible. An assertion of the self, a commitment, is essential if the self is to have any reality.

—ROLLO MAY

W HENEVER WE ARE FACED WITH CHANGE—even predictable change, even chosen change—it is unsettling. Change involves risk and all risk is disruptive. When we consider the risk side of change, it helps to find mentors, friends, and counselors who will listen, advise, and care for us in our time of vulnerability.

Some pleasurable consequences of change can be the support we find from others. We also can feel supported from inside: a heightened awareness of beauty, justice, goodness, joy. The rewards of increased self-awareness and acceptance bring us to our inner home—our true Self.

However, before obtaining these rewards we often pass through a time when our fears surface. Some fears may be about making a mistake or stepping out of culturally approved roles. Often we have fears about financial concerns. When we make changes, we might fear embarrassment or ridicule from our peers. Sometimes we fear that the changes we are considering may create dissension within the family.

The people I interviewed came to recognize some of the risks involved in making their life changes. They evaluated what the consequences of their decisions might be, not only for themselves but also for those close to them.

One woman stated it well. After returning to school in adulthood and entering a profession, she spoke of things being scarier, having left the protected environment of home. Many people she associated with didn't quite know how to respond to her now. Her husband had approved of her former role in the home, but the changes put a strain on their relationship.

When a woman steps out of her supportive role in the home and begins an outside challenge, husbands and children find their lives affected. She is turning her emotional and physical energy in other directions. Families respond in different ways to these challenges, but one familiar way is to be irritated with one's mate or mom—feeling abandoned, neglected. The men I interviewed did not have to contend with this dynamic—all but one woman did.

Women who are in the process of change often carry guilt because they are breaking out of cultural patterns, and they feel selfish when they put their desires and wants in the forefront. For some families, however, having the wife and mother begin a new role outside the home proves to be a maturing process for children—and even for the husband. Family members become more resourceful by taking increased responsibility for themselves. Sometimes the family rallies around and becomes the team to cheer mom on in her new life. I have been to several graduation ceremonies where families who were proud of their graduating mates and mothers waved banners and cheered, "Good work, Mom!" or "Congratulations!" as she walked across the stage for her diploma.

Other women have found that their marriages suffered when things changed. The women that I interviewed did not succeed as well as the men in finding family support for their expanded generative moves.

Liana's Risks and Consequences

Before her near-death experience, Liana had enjoyed success and personal acclaim in the art world. Her dramatic experience influenced her to take her painting in a new direction. Liana recalled that only a few critics recognized something exciting emerging in her new artistic explorations. She came under fire from some Chicago newspaper critics for using art for spiritual exploration. That hurt.

As time passed, her husband, who had supported her art career wholeheartedly, chose not to join Liana on her new journey. He had enjoyed the managing, traveling, and entertaining that went with promoting Liana's career, but when she changed, gradually dropping her art, they had less and less in common. Ten years later they were divorced.

Liana entered extensive training with doctors like W. Brugh Joy and Stanislov Grof. She now helps clients facilitate their natural healing powers through visualization, meditation, music, therapeutic touch and more. She would not go back to her old life. But even so she warned, "Stepping out of culturally defined behaviors is a risk. It requires a high degree of faith."

"There Are Lots of Times When I Wish I Didn't See Injustice"

Another member of the group and a risk taker whom I haven't yet mentioned is Jack, a chaplain at a Big Ten university. Educated in the finest institutions available, he is a combination intellectual and outdoor man in his early forties with clear, penetrating eyes. He hates wearing suits, preferring jeans and an open-necked shirt.

Jack has a passion for peace, justice, and God, which has led him to step out in defense of those who are victims of prejudice, poverty, or war. He told me about some difficult times: "I get lots of flack and many people don't like what I'm doing." One university fired him before his first day of work because they received letters from people accusing him of being a communist. "I had been arrested several times for my antiwar demonstrations, and people assumed I was anti-American. They didn't even give me a hearing. This was hard—especially on my wife."

On another occasion, Jack promised his wife that he would keep a low profile in his new university position. However, a few days later a black co-ed came to him weeping because a young black friend had been convicted of raping a white woman and was sentenced to forty years in jail. "He didn't do it" she told Jack. "Please, can you help?" Jack interviewed the prosecuting attorney who warned him to let the issue go and not interfere or he would be asking for trouble! Others in the legal system said, "A black man is lucky not to get the death penalty; there is nothing we can do." Jack was soon fired from the university for getting involved in this and other similar situations.

"There are lots of times when I wish I didn't see injustice," Jack admitted to me. But he does, and seeing, he feels compelled to act regardless of personal consequences. He and a few friends have been committed to nuclear disarmament for many years. They know that a considerable portion of our tax dollars goes to continuously building more nuclear arms. As a protest, they withhold the percentage of their taxes that would go to this buildup and deposit it into a separate account. When and if the government decides to prosecute them, they will use the fund to defend themselves. For the past ten years, the IRS has chosen to overlook their action.

George's Fulfillment

George, the dentist, traveled at his own expense and donated extended periods of time to clinics in South Africa, Central America, and Korea. When he began his volunteer work, he found it frustrating because the need was so great. The crowds who waited outside the clinic in the hope of getting their teeth attended to broke his heart. Gradually, over the years, however, George could see improvement as volunteers cooperated with one another and donated skills, supplies, and equipment to the challenge.

George served in some places when the political situation was touchy. On one occasion, he and his wife flew to Zimbabwe (then Rhodesia) to work in a medical compound. Things were tense. Army patrols guarded the hospital grounds. Wounded from both sides were brought in for emergency treatment. No one asked questions. George said:

> It was like a M*A*S*H situation only without the
> women and wine. But the people you work with are so
> tremendous—it's unbelievable. You're with them one
> hour and you feel you've known them all your life.

93

They have such a sense of humor, they're so flexible—
you never know today what you'll have to do tomorrow.
They have developed resourcefulness; they know how to
fix things. It is so heartwarming!

Back home, however, people didn't understand. "Most
people think I am out of my mind. They say, 'Well, what are
you going over there for, to work? At your own expense?
What thanks do you get?'" George loves his life of adventure
and service and gets thanks aplenty. His wife loves it to, and
it adds a wonderful dimension to their marriage.

Discouragement Comes

Bill's experiences while attempting to organize a vehicle
to provide loans to help develop small businesses in the
Third World provides another example of the risks that
generative people take. He was on the verge of the highest
financial earning period of his life when he reversed tracks
and became a full-time volunteer. But there was nothing of
the martyr or do-gooder in Bill—this is something to note.
Generative people do what they do because they *want* to do
it. Bill assured me that giving up the big money was of no
consequence. However, he felt he needed to discuss it with
his children, so he and Helen called a family conference
and asked their young adult children how they felt about
having their potential inheritance cut off. They received
their children's blessing.

The real surprise for Bill was how many of his acquaintances and friends tried to discourage him and his dream.
Bill had no idea whether his idea of making small business
loans would work. All he knew was that he had to try.

Roberta spoke of hiding the fact that she attended a local community college after her children were all in school. She knew her family would make fun of her, but she spoke also of deeper risks. When one dares to acknowledge what is really happening, then depression and discouragement can follow. The problems can seem so big and the resources so small. Roberta on several occasions asked herself, "What can one little person do?"

"It Was the Beginning of Freedom and Independence"

Barbara had lived a life bound in many ways by her blindness. She yearned for independence. In her teen years, Barbara learned how to live with a Seeing Eye dog.

> It was such a thrill with my first dog, just to go to the drug store and buy some simple thing—I think it was a lipstick that I bought. I was so thrilled—I was just walking on air! I had done it by myself! It was the real beginning of freedom and independence and getting around and being able to do the things I wanted to do on my own. Now I can walk down the street at a good clip with my dog and feel so free and confident!

The experience was a turning point in her life. She graduated from college with a degree in music and played the piano professionally, she married and raised four children, she worked with the Chicago Symphony's children's program traveling to schools all over the Chicago area teaching and preparing children for the coming concerts. She also was a radio announcer for five years on a classical music program, and she is very active in her church.

95

Barbara and her Seeing Eye dog are a familiar sight on trains and in buses in her area. Barbara is a widow now and finds widowhood especially difficult because in many ways her husband was her eyes as well as her mate.

Political Shortsightedness

Peter, whose young son died, is clear about his purpose in life: to do what he can in helping others have a chance at a good life. He has seen how shortsightedness and lack of caring for humanity at the governmental level bring disaster to many. For example, he believes that the starvation in Ethiopia could have been avoided.

> When Jack Kennedy was president, he proposed a United Nations Development Decade. If we'd followed through on that program, there wouldn't have been a lack of food in Africa. We have modern techniques—the little state of Israel has learned a drip system and converted deserts. . . . Why not Ethiopia? There was no human appreciation of the fact that these people had no destiny unless we intervened. They were part of the world! People block it out—well, I haven't!

Peter does not enjoy golf and gin rummy games in sunnier climes, where many people in his age group are found. "I used to play golf. It's boring; I quit my two clubs. How long can you play golf and think you're somebody?" Peter prefers to think and read and often mediates between groups with different viewpoints. "I feel it is a compliment that warring factions ask me to mediate."

Peter sometimes believes the impossible. He believes that dreams lengthen your life. "What you want may seem like an impossible dream, but if you go one inch at a

96

time . . . " he counsels. Some of his mediating tasks can appear impossible; for example, the negotiations between the Palestinians and the Jews: "I believe we can have peace in the Middle East, and I'm one of the few damn fools that does!" He thrives on the challenges of the world.

Transition times come to us again and again, some major, others less so. Each time, these three components will probably exist: the pivotal event or invasive event, the sense of call or purpose, and the willingness to risk, evaluate, and accept the consequences of our decisions.

CHAPTER SEVEN

A Delightful Quality
of Personality

They are devoted, working at something, something which is very precious to them—some calling or vocation in the old priestly sense. They are working at something that they love, so that the work-joy dichotomy in them disappears.

—ABRAHAM MASLOW

EXPERTS SAY THAT AS MANY AS ninety-five percent of Americans do not enjoy the work they do. Unlike Maslow's description, their joy is in their off-hours—their work is a burden. In a culture that is supposedly so civilized and wealthy, what could this mean? One thing it means is that unhappiness is more widespread than we care to admit.

Some observers of our culture speak of existential dread; others talk of stress, low-grade depression, and anxiety. Could it be that we have been sold a bill of goods about what makes for happiness and life satisfaction? Have we bought the hype that we have to be slim, rich, and powerful to have a life worth living?

99

It is a major task to bring our personal, political and spiritual ideals into harmony with our careers or jobs and is one of the by-products of generativity, of successful living. Even if you do not have the ideal job, you can change the dynamics of your life by giving your present work more careful attention. Generativity is, among other things, an attitude, and by embracing a more generous and positive attitude you are inviting the next step in your development while easing the difficulties in your present situation. A positive attitude is a deeply held commitment aligned with the truth of your life and it means learning to discover your vital desires—which come from your inner core. "Let the beauty of what you love be what you do," the ancient poet Rumi counseled.

The lives of the people I interviewed bear testimony to the fact that inner changes can bring about useful outer changes. For them the work-joy dichotomy disappeared. Why? Because they began to do what they loved and they loved what they did, and this truth shone in their personalities.

Generativity is not a destination, but a process of maturing successfully, and with happiness. This delightful quality of personality was evident in all the people I interviewed. The older ones displayed it even more than the younger ones. Clearly, something so valuable needs time and nourishment to flourish and develop.

Maturing generativity appears to have four characteristics. The first is the special view of life and of the world these men and women had formed to explain their experiences. Second is the caring behaviors they engaged in and the rewards that accompanied their chosen activities. Third is self-understanding. And fourth is the capacity to be filled with dreams and hopes, which emerged strongly in the interviews like shining rays of light.

A *Special View of Life and the World*

These women and men had formed a philosophy of life that validated their experiences and helped them make sense of the complexities and paradoxes inherent in life. We see life as both good and bad, helpful and sabotaging, healthy and diseased—this can be confusing. We experience these polarities within ourselves as well. The people I interviewed had struggled with this confusion and disharmony and had learned to live with disparities.

All had formed theories about the meaning of life that centered on spiritual insights, disciplines, and traditions, whether or not these had been part of their early training. They believed in a benevolent force or Being who loved and cared for the world and for all individuals. Some spoke of the Mother aspects of God and the need to correct the imbalance toward a male-dominated image of divinity. They believed that the small events of their lives had meaning in a larger picture; they spoke of the oneness of all creation, that all people are children of the same Mother-Father creative source and are sisters and brothers.

They also shared a concern over the ineffectiveness and the direction of governments worldwide. They have great hopes that humanity will avoid such devastations as nuclear holocaust or the rape of the earth. Most felt that the "people" are better than their governments and change must come from grassroots commitment.

It was clear that these women and men felt a trust in the life process itself and were deeply committed to a loving, spiritual Being, as they understood that mystery. They felt this presence wanted them to be active in making the world a fairer, safer place.

Caring Behaviors and Their Rewards

The useful resource of personality we call caring grows naturally from the activities associated with the development of generativity. The joyful elements of caring bubbled out as the women and men spoke of their work and their lives. Their joy and laughter rested on strength within, which manifested outwardly as gentleness. They had positive accepting attitudes about themselves, their families, their failures, their successes, and their futures.

Many were known for their larger commitments to serving and caring, but the small opportunities to show love were also viewed as important. Barbara put it this way: "Simple ways to give count, too. The happiness and joy of living is in giving of myself, whether babysitting with my grandchildren or other ordinary activities." Others spoke of caring for and taking pleasure in everyday life: doing simple chores, maintaining gardens and homes, building a cabin in the woods by hand. Lewis said that his writing feeds him. "I'm writing for myself as much as for the public. I get genuine love from other people which I pass on." Peter affirmed: "I enjoy the challenges of the world. I have a lot of vigor; I do what I do because I like it!"

The many joyful aspects of caring were balanced by quick tears and even suffering because their involvement sometimes risked their financial stability, personal safety, convenience, or family harmony.

In Peter's and Roberta's stories, as well as in Bill's, it is easy to pick out the polarities of suffering and joy in their

102

experiences of caring. Jack, the university chaplain who is so passionately committed to justice, felt acutely the pain of his work—even though he deeply wants to do it. Jack said that the pain he carries inside because of what he does and the hurting people he is involved with is sometimes overwhelming. He is currently working to change a high crime neighborhood to a place where people can find work, food, clothes, housing, and spiritual and emotional support.

> I carry pain very poorly. I carry tons of pain but
> I don't have a good way to let it go. It really hurts a lot
> —working with people—and the kinds of things I do.
> I need to get away and be healed. I like to spend time
> alone in the woods. I spend lots of time praying and
> I do a lot of singing—something I learned from the
> native Americans—sort of responding to nature in
> a song.

Self-Understanding

Self-understanding refers to how the men and women viewed their backgrounds, their value shifts, their own personalities (both positive and negative components), their mistakes, and their successes. They made sense of their lives and successfully integrated all the elements.

As they moved further along in the process of maturing generativity, they became aware of their changing values. And, finally, they spoke of the deep need to spend time alone, to reflect, to experience creative, restoring solitude.

Roberta's journey of self-understanding, for example, included coming to terms with a time in her life when she went into a "hate thing" over racial prejudice and injustices. She began to hate the white race just as she felt she had been hated. This feeling grew until it polluted her attitudes, making her angry and depressed. Finally she confessed it to her mentor, a white nun, and gradually let it go through some forgiveness processes. When it finally lifted, Roberta felt as though a heavy burden had been taken off her shoulders.

Releasing our attitudes of criticism and intolerance toward others brings a light-hearted free feeling of vitality— and is so worth the effort. When we judge others and cast them out of our hearts, we sentence ourselves to feel like the outcast. I was thinking about this one day when a squirrel outside my window became a parable.

OUTCAST FRIEND

Furless body, fluffy tail, illness left its mark
January's squirrel shivered
Beneath yesterday's bird feeder—searching in the snow

Earlier birds and squirrels
Eating well, went on their way
Then did the needy one
Pick among the hulls
Shunning and shunned

My heart nudged me
I found some walnuts to toss
She ran away
Her plump cousins came instead
How like life, I mused
Some know how to find, some shiver alone

Today on my porch rail
The outcast squirrel hunched
Our eyes held a long, long time
Slowly opening the door, I tossed more nuts

She scurried up a tree
But soon returned and feasted well

I felt communion with a friend
I too have felt outcast—
And now have learned to feast.

Some of the people in the group chose to simplify their lifestyles, to free themselves from the care and burden of too many material possessions. Giving up spacious homes or country clubs is not necessary to generativity, but for some it was not a hard choice when the timing was right. As Bill put it, after selling his new dream house to move to Washington, D.C. where his generativity was calling him, "There was no trauma involved." Giving things up should not be done, however, if one is still attached to them, because time and energy will be spent either regretting the loss or trying to recover the loss.

When these men and women spoke of the need to be alone, to find quiet, they echoed a deep need in my heart. I find that if I miss my quiet times too often, I become irritable and difficult to live with. One person who is in great demand spoke of "disappearing for a time." Others loved to walk outdoors, taking time to think and enjoy nature. Another spoke of needing quiet to gain spiritual depth.

Several people felt they were not getting enough time for themselves and that this was one of their biggest needs. One businessman struggles with giving himself permission just to *be*, rather than always doing and producing.

These people value self-understanding. Many have had some therapy to facilitate the process; others had mentors or wise older friends. Most spent time with personal journals, religious disciplines, educational strategies, self-help and growth groups. Whatever their path, these men and women were concerned with developing ever greater self-knowledge, and also cultivated relationships with others who were journeying on a similar path.

Dreams and Hopes

Hopes and dreams varied from small joys and accomplishments like Elloah's, who had started piano lessons and had wanted to play a carol by Christmas, to more ambitious goals like Peter's, who wants to "do something to help people of goodwill in the world come to the negotiating table in a spirit of reconciliation instead of confrontation."

Dreams and hopes on the personal level centered around caring for children and grandchildren. Some spoke of their feelings of failure as young parents to care for their children well, but now that their caring skills had developed they invested much more of themselves in their adult children, grandchildren, nieces, nephews, and others.

These generative women and men wanted to travel, to enjoy good health, to garden, write books, hike, learn to cook. One wanted to become a bird watcher, another to try snorkeling or play the guitar. They wanted to try their hand at painting or sketching, take piano lessons, write an autobiography for the grandchildren, trace their family trees or write poetry. They planned on continuing to develop even greater leadership in the coming generation. Many wanted their dreams to continue beyond their lifetimes. Roberta voiced the hope for someone to share her dream and take over in the years ahead. "I hope I am building leadership. I'd hate to see this work die if I'm not around."

All see the future as challenging. Some spoke of the limited time left to them and of things they wanted to accomplish in that time. Most spoke of life continuing beyond the death of the body and felt this life was only a small, but vital, part of a continuing drama. Death was seen to be a doorway, a birth, to a different dimension. Several were going through more transitions. One forty-one-year-old man was considering a career change that would involve further schooling.

There's No Going Back!

Maturing generativity includes the process of forming a world view to encompass the complexity of individual experiences and needs, and adapting and readapting that structure or belief system to meet the demands of change. It means developing healthier capacities to care wisely, and letting go of the need to control while learning to trust one's self, life, God, and unanswered questions. Generativity is a process of shifting values and changing lifestyles.

In spite of the fears, risks, and difficulties of the paths that they chose, these men and women knew they would never return to old ways of doing things or old values. Their futures are hopeful and dream-filled—there is no going back for them.

PART II

Through
the
golden
door:
the
path
to
successful
aging

Introduction

Wᴴᴱɴ ɪ ꜰɪʀꜱᴛ ᴛʀɪᴇᴅ ᴛᴏ ᴡʀɪᴛᴇ this section, I found myself completely blocked. I felt inadequate to the
task of describing practical, realistic ways to cultivate generativity in one's life. The block was a big one and
forced me to lay the manuscript aside for more than two
years.

Then one morning as I lay in bed in the place between
waking and sleeping, a powerful image came to me. The
obstruction seemed like a great, dark, stone wall similar to
those that surround medieval castles. I couldn't see over it;
I couldn't see around it. It was indeed formidable. I remembered Robert Frost's words, "Something there is that doesn't
love a wall." I felt powerless next to this one.

I looked again at the image of the dark, stone wall, and I
was stunned to find that at the ground level of this great barrier a small golden door had appeared. Dwarfed by the huge
structure around it, it was just the right size for me to enter.
The door was penetrated by a golden light that glowed
through the old wood like the beams of a flashlight held
against a hand. Light streamed around its edges, around the
curved top, down the sides, and under the bottom. I was too
overcome to open the door yet, but I arose, felt a benediction on my work, and began this section of the book.

The path into successful aging has such a doorway leading us to tasks we must undertake, attitudes and values we
need to release, strengths and qualities we need to develop.
The door is there for each of us as we negotiate the middle

years—in fact one door leads to another. Part Two presents material that can be useful as you consider the door that opens into your future.

I have a friend who went through the experience of her father dying. She faithfully visited him, trying to soothe and comfort him, but he would not be comforted. Shortly before his death, in a moment of clarity, he began to speak softly. She leaned close. "Ever since I was a young man, I had a sense that God had something special for me to do—but, well, the years passed and life pressed in and I never discovered what it was. Now I'll never know. I feel so empty . . . I feel like I've not really lived." We can learn from these words. Each of us has a deep need to feel that our lives have counted, that we have found and fulfilled our purpose.

All our lives are important and each is a vital link in the vast web of life. When we do not find and fulfill our part, there is a hole, a torn place in the pattern. Too many holes and tears will hurt the pattern deeply.

We will consider the qualities needed to move through our golden door—awareness, humility, patience, perseverance, trust, hope, and love. These great strengths are cultivated and lived out in relationship with our true Self first, and then with others. We will look at the process of self-understanding, and face the challenges of intimate relationships and family interactions. Children are the future—we will discuss how to cultivate strength in the next generation. The little child we once were often wrestles with the adult we are now. A compassionate relationship with our inner child of yesterday will touch the springs of our playfulness and creativity today.

We'll see how our mini-collapses and crises contribute to our lives. Times of depression, anxiety, discouragement, and disillusionment demand our introspection. These painful times teach us what is authentic in ourselves so we can be released from attitudes, beliefs, and behaviors that no longer serve us. Like the release that came to so many when the Berlin wall came down, when our personal walls come down we open ourselves to new life and new freedom. And like the changes coming so fast in Eastern Europe and in the Middle East, there will be uncertainty and chaos as old things pass away and new things form.

Increased freedom brings increased responsibility. As we go through the golden door we will recognize choices, and we will take responsibility for the way our lives are going.

Facing death usually comes to us first through our grandparents—but often we are so young that we let this experience slip on by. In midlife, however, when we see frailty and death coming to our parents, it is not so easy to avoid the realization that we, too, will die. This time can become a major transition time for us, reshaping our priorities, teaching us to focus our energies on vital interests. There are many gifts for us as we experience this process called dying.

When we are on the path that is right for us, it is as though the way before us has been prepared—and we are surprised by joy. We trust the life process because it becomes trustworthy. Some of the common themes shared by the world's great religions bring us awareness of connections to our higher Self and connections to others who can light the way for us.

It is a challenging journey, the second half of life, requiring honesty, integrity, perseverance, openness, and much more. It also offers great rewards—even miracles—of which we have not dared to dream. Welcome to the heroic journey—the way through the golden door.

113

CHAPTER EIGHT

"I Make a Difference"

... Are you the keen thinker who scrutinizes his [her] inner self, discarding that which is useless, outworn and evil, but preserving that which is useful and good? If so, you are as manna to the hungry, and as cool, clear water to the thirsty.

—Kahlil Gibran

YOUR LIFE IS INCREDIBLY IMPORTANT. Your life is special and makes a difference in the larger scheme of things. You have a destiny and a unique contribution to make, and, as you begin to answer your particular call, you will find you are supported, guided, and loved all the way. You will meet people who have found the golden door in the second half of life, and you will journey together, crossing the threshold into new terrain.

We receive many rewards when our decisions are life-nurturing and make positive differences in other lives. When we do our inner work in the second half of life and do the sorting that Gibran alludes to, we can truly give to others.

The Dalai Lama, who won the Nobel Peace Prize in 1989, challenges our thinking. He recognizes that we live in crucial times and encourages us to feel it is an honor to be alive today. This is a refreshing perspective, and further highlights our obligation to contribute. Many appear to hope that the problems facing our planet today will be solved through technological expertise. Others seem to think that things will work out if we develop peace and goodwill. Both positions have some truth to them, but more is needed.

If we reflect on our lives, we will see how we can make a difference in ourselves, our families, our friendships, and the extended community. Do we dare see the suffering and danger all around and will we have the wisdom and courage to get involved? Will we notice where we have personal leverage and how we can best contribute? Becoming more aware and involved will also enable us to reap the satisfying rewards that come with thoughtful action.

The Hundredth Monkey Phenomenon

The value of one life and its power to make a critical difference for many is illustrated by a controversial but fascinating scientific experiment with the Japanese monkey, *Macaca fuscata,* which was conducted in the 1950s on the island of Koshima. The Hundredth Monkey Phenomenon lends support to the intriguing possibility that when a critical number of monkeys engaged in a new behavior, monkeys across the sea suddenly emulated that behavior. Transferring this concept to the human world, it indicates that our minds are interconnected—that the influence of one life transformed in a positive way can be felt at some deep resonating level by the larger group.

Contemporary scientific research validates this concept that mystics and prophets of all faiths and in all times have intuitively known. Our thoughts, beliefs, and behaviors send out signals that affect others positively or negatively on levels of which we are only vaguely aware.

Physics Agrees: We Are All One

Unity is being recognized in unexpected circles. Spiritual wisdom and science are beginning to meet at the growing edge of physics. The concept that we are all one is now being talked about among physicists like Gary Zukov and Fritjof Capra, who put some of this thinking in layperson's language in their still somewhat difficult (for me) books. They describe something of what "new physics" is recognizing.

Quantum theory, subatomic particle physics, and Bell's theorem attempt to describe the phenomenon that spiritual wisdom has recognized—an interdependence and connectedness of all things extending into the whole universe. What appear to be separate parts are actually connected in a most intimate and immediate way.

For example, subatomic particles seem to know instantaneously what decisions are made elsewhere. Bell's theorem demands that we rethink the conventional scientific ideas of the nature of the material world and instead consider connections that more resemble telepathic communications. The metaphor of the dance illustrates that everything is connected, communicating instantaneously all the time. This system of communicating parts includes you and me—we are an integral part of the whole dance of life.

Our Thoughts Communicate: Madeleine and Her Father

Madeleine's story illustrates the idea that our thoughts communicate in ways we may not fully understand. Madeleine

117

was in her forties when she decided to let go of some destructive attitudes she was holding against her father. The abusive relationship started in early childhood. Over the years she began to realize that her relationships with men suffered because of the anger and grievances she was carrying. She became convinced that she needed to come to terms with the past to be free in the present.

Sarah, an older, wise confidante, heard her story. Madeleine revealed her pain and sorrow and anger while Sarah asked questions and provided a loving heart space.

"I'm ready to forgive my father," Madeleine announced one day. This was a big step for her. She no longer felt the need to hang on to her sadness or to get back at him.

"Are you sure, Madeleine?" Sarah asked. "Sometimes we tend to forgive too fast, before we realize just how much it hurt."

"Yes, I'm sure. But how? Should I try to track him down? Is it always necessary to tell someone who has hurt you exactly what you feel so you can find resolution?"

"No," replied Sarah, "in fact sometimes it would just reenact the original pain of rejection. Sometimes the other person is not able to handle such a confrontation. But there are no rules. Each situation is unique and has to be approached individually."

Sarah suggested a practical forgiveness exercise. For about fifteen minutes a day for one week Madeleine was to write on a sheet of paper fifty times, "I, Madeleine, forgive you, father, for everything" and then see what happened. Sarah explained that by writing it down, Madeleine was putting the forgiveness process through her muscles, which would help her body to release its tension around painful childhood memories.

118

Madeleine accepted the challenge. She bought colored pens and wrote the sentences in blocks of ten, each block in a different color. She noticed some physical responses to her writing meditations. One day she felt nauseated; other times she felt a sense of relief. She had particularly vivid dreams, which she wrote down.

At the end of the week, Madeleine brought her pages of colorful forgiveness statements to her friend. Sarah, with tears in her eyes, expressed her joy over the true art and beauty of Madeleine's process.

Two months passed and it was Christmas time. Madeleine and her family took a trip. When they returned home, the mail contained an envelope with an unfamiliar address. It was from Madeleine's father. Her hands trembled as she opened the letter. It was brief, almost like a telegram.

Dear Madeleine,

Your father needs to be forgiven so he can sleep nights. Please.

Love,
Dad

Tears sprang to Madeleine's eyes. She never thought he would acknowledge that he had hurt her, let alone ask for forgiveness. It was a miracle—but she would proceed slowly. Sarah explained to her the idea that as humans we have the power to lose or bind each other by our thoughts. Madeleine's forgiveness work had had great power, not only in Madeleine's life, but also apparently in her father's.

Eventually Madeleine and her father reconnected. The family helped him celebrate his eightieth birthday, but Madeleine had to accept that the relationship would never be a close one.

Nevertheless, her story exemplifies the idea that we may be more connected to others than we imagine, that our thoughts may affect others across many miles. Forgiveness towards others can liberate at subtle levels and is a major task in the second half of life. Clinging to grievances will cast dark shadows. In full forgiveness our hearts can feel cleansed, enlivened, healthy. With every healed relationship, more light and love come into the world.

If healthy love can send healing and goodwill to others, it also follows that destructive thoughts will send out harmful messages. It is worth pondering the concept that what we send out comes back to us. The karmic teachings of Buddhists and Hindus speak of the far-reaching effects of our lives.

By the second half of life, we have established patterns of thought and belief, some helpful, some not. These often operate unconsciously. However, paying close attention to what we say and how we react will make us aware of these old patterns. Our children, for example, often trigger them and we are surprised to hear ourselves saying the same things our parents said to us. This is a moment of opportunity. Do we really believe what we just said? Do we really want to hang on to that thought or attitude? In this opportunity for self-examination, we can scrutinize our inner selves, and discard that which is outworn or destructive.

When we begin to recognize, examine, and take responsibility for the quality of our thoughts, accepting the far-reaching impact they may carry, we see just how unruly they often are. The ancient wisdom of Socrates counsels, "The unexamined life is not worth living." Carefully monitoring and choosing the thoughts we give ourselves and others will contribute immeasurably to the happiness, love, and compassion in our own lives first, then naturally spreading to others.

Teddy and Ms. Thompson

The story about Teddy and Ms. Thompson was told by sociologist Anthony Compolo, Jr. during a local Chicago TV program. It illustrates one woman's journey through her golden door of heart healing. As she examined her life, her heart accused her, and rightly so. She listened to herself and changed her attitudes, the way she related to others, and her work as a teacher. These changes encouraged one little boy who was hurting. As the years passed and one choice led to another, Ms. Thompson received more heart gifts than she could have imagined—and so will we.

I have a friend. She is a school teacher, Ms. Thompson. Some years ago, when her new fifth-grade class came in, Ms. Thompson looked over the students and saw one little boy she disliked immediately. Sometimes he had a surly look; at other times he stared into space with his mouth hanging half open. He was uninterested in class activities.

When Ms. Thompson marked his papers, she got a certain perverse delight in putting Xs next to the wrong answers. When she wrote an F at the top of the paper, she did it with a flair. Ms. Thompson should have known better. She had Teddy's records from previous teachers:

First grade: "Teddy shows promise by work and attitude, but poor home situation."

Second grade: "Teddy could do better. Mother terminally ill. He receives little help at home."

Third Grade: "Teddy is a pleasant boy, helpful, but too serious. He is a slow learner. Mother passed away this year."

Fourth Grade: "Teddy is very slow, well behaved. Father shows no interest."

Christmas came and all the boys and girls brought their presents for the teacher. She opened them one by one and finally came to a present from Teddy. It was wrapped in brown paper and held together with Scotch tape. When she tore the paper, out fell an ugly rhinestone bracelet with half the stones missing and a bottle of cheap perfume partly used.

The children began to titter, but Ms. Thompson had enough sense to put some of the perfume on each of her wrists and hold them up for the children to smell, saying "Isn't it lovely?"

At the end of the day when the other children had left, little Teddy lingered behind. He came up to her and said, "Ms. Thompson, you smell just like my mother did. And her bracelet looks real nice on you, too. I'm glad you liked my present."

When he left, Ms. Thompson's heart accused her. She saw her poverty of spirit toward Teddy and others. She got down on her knees and asked for forgiveness. She prayed for a new vision of her life's purpose.

The next day, when the children came to class, they came to a transformed classroom and a transformed teacher, a place of warmth, caring, and beauty. And Teddy Stoddard began to learn. By the end of the school year he had caught up with most of the students and was ahead of some of them.

Ms. Thompson didn't hear from Teddy for many years. Then one day she got the first of three short notes: "Dear Ms. Thompson, I wanted you to be the first to know. I will be graduating second in my high school class next month." Four years later: "Dear Ms. Thompson, I wanted you to be the first to know. I was just informed

I will be graduating first in my class. The university has not been easy, but I liked it."

Four years later: "Dear Ms. Thompson, I wanted you to be the first to know—as of today I am Theodore J. Stoddard, M.D., how about that? I'm going to be married in July, the 27th to be exact. I want you to come and sit where my mother would have sat if my mother was alive. I have no family but you now. Dad died last year."

Ms. Thompson sat where Teddy's mother would have sat. And the irony of the story is that today the Stoddard family is the only family that she has.

Miracles happen when even one person changes her thoughts and attitudes. As Ms. Thompson learned to care for her pupils with greater wisdom, she created a more positive, less lonely future for herself. Who was the giver and who the receiver? The beauty of generativity is that it is a mutually beneficial way of life.

The Conscious Way

Buddhists speak of two types of minds, the skilled mind and the unskilled or ignorant mind. The former brings about the overcoming of suffering. The person with the skilled mind serves others with ever-increasing love and joy. The unskilled or untrained mind unwittingly contributes to suffering and confusion, making more problems than it knows how to handle.

Jesus spoke of these two groups in the metaphor of the broad way, which many take, and the narrow way, which is harder to find. The broad, easier way leads toward unconscious living, comfort seeking, self-justification, and short-term pleasures that result in love-starved lifestyles that hurt. The narrow, more difficult way leads to increased awareness of truth—clearing away debris that blocks the flow from inexhaustible fountains of love and compassion. The narrow way requires far-sightedness and leads to long-term enjoyments.

As more of us embrace the ability to see with long-term vision, we are making a difference in our own and others' lives. In midlife, we need to learn the importance of caring for the quality of society, of earth, air, and water, which we pass on to the generations to come.

The Laws of Nature

One evening my husband David and I sat taking in a spectacular sunset over Lake Michigan. We witnessed the panorama of color, felt the fall winds blowing off the lake, heard the music of waves, and felt the mystery of great beauty. He said, "I don't have the arrogance to doubt that there is a Higher Greatness which has made all this and has made us." That statement echoed in my heart. The splendor and awesome power of nature rules our ultimate fate on this planet. Nature's laws must be obeyed or we will reap painful consequences.

Today the effects of our abuses of our home, the earth, are haunting us on every side. Dan Goleman, who regularly writes on behavioral sciences for *The New York Times,* spoke at a conference sponsored by the East-West Foundation. He noted that the big news of today seldom gets the attention in the press that it deserves. The big news? We live on a dying planet.

- The greenhouse effect may raise temperatures worldwide and produce widespread crop failures and famine.

- The ozone layer—our protection from the sun—is threatened.
- Five percent of the world's people produce twenty-five percent of the noxious chemicals polluting air, water, and soil.
- Rain forests, which are a rich source of oxygen, are being destroyed at the rate of fifty acres a minute.
- Our earth family is so dysfunctional that forty thousand of its children age five and under die every day, most from preventable causes like starvation and diarrhea.
- Worldwide we are accumulating nuclear weapons at a cost of $1 million a minute.

The list could go on and on. Our planet, which has been evolving for millions of years, is dying in the sense that it may no longer be able to support human and other forms of life. The earth will go on, but will we still maintain our niche on it? Cosmonaut Sigmund Jahn recognized humanity's awesome challenge:

Before I flew I was already aware of how small and vulnerable our planet is; but only when I saw it from space, in all its ineffable beauty and fragility, did I realize that humankind's most urgent task is to cherish and preserve it for future generations.

We need a deep ecology, warns anthropologist Joan Halifax, a world view that recognizes the earth is a living web, a kind of complex community. Each part of the earth system has its place. If we pollute our air supply, soil our rivers and lakes, or take down our giant trees, we are committing suicide as a species. Halifax noted that we human beings are the pathogens in the earth's immune system and only we have the power to change this.

125

Many thoughtful people are uniting and forming grassroots organizations to address these problems. Alan Durning, in *The State of the World,* wrote of such community movements being enacted internationally. In Germany the Green Party is fostering public environmental awareness; in India strong Gandhian self-help traditions promote tree planting, social welfare, and much more; in Zimbabwe, since the transfer to black rule in 1980, thousands of women's community gardens and small-farmer groups have formed.

Ultimate responsibility for the future of the earth and its peoples rests with individuals like you and me. Six of us recently returned from a hiking trip in the African wilderness. Tears came to my eyes more than once as I felt the majesty of the wild that is still available in Botswana and Zimbabwe. I wrote:

AFRICAN BENEDICTION

Timeless, abundant, and wild
Is the Kalahari
Forty million years the rhino roams
Monolith in the bushveld
Squinting out at me

Wild things have a place here
Diversity
Space here
Everything useful to something
For something

A lioness kills for her young
Birds first scream the news
Baboons shriek
Prancing Impalas grunt warnings

Hyenas, loping, move in
Vultures hover
All in turn
No waste

Elephants implacable, munch on
Great rounds against the sky
Lilac-breasted roller birds glide
Rainbows in feathers

Rose-red the sand
Golden grasses bend
Mopane trees keep watch
Mystical Baobabs, ancient, know

My too-civilized soul stretches
In a world all but lost
And at some essential, animating core
I find my place in the family of life.

Native American cultures have always understood "the family of life." They had a deep respect for the earth and for each animal that gave its life for their food and clothing. They honored the very ground they walked upon as their mother. One of the sacred songs sung by the Ojai Foundation, a community in California dedicated to living in harmony with nature, speaks of this:

The earth is our mother, we must take care of her,
The earth is our mother we must take care of her . . .
Her sacred ground we walk upon with every step we take,
Her sacred ground we walk upon with every step we take.

Astronaut Edgar Mitchell, in another perspective, felt he was given a glimpse of Divinity when he viewed our planet from space.

127

> Suddenly from behind the rim of the moon, in a long, slow-motion moment of immense majesty, there emerges a sparkling blue and white jewel, a light, delicate sky-blue sphere laced with slowly swirling veils of white, rising gradually like a small pearl in a thick sea of black mystery. It takes more than a moment to fully realize this is Earth . . . home.

A human revolution in attitude is needed to nurture our Earth home back to health, and for such a revolution we need the expertise and generativity of those of us in our power years. The internal reflection and spiritual awareness that naturally arises during this time of life can powerfully contribute to the solutions of our problems.

Being Real Is Essential

The spiritual journey becomes increasingly compelling in the middle years as we wake up to what is essential—the open heart that loves well. The nature of the quest for what is real, for one's inner core where we are all connected, is caught in the children's story *The Velveteen Rabbit.*

> "What is REAL?" asked the Rabbit one day, when they were lying side by side near the nursery fender . . .
> "Does it mean having things that buzz inside you and a stick-out handle?"
> "Real isn't how you are made," said the Skin Horse. "It's a thing that happens to you. When a child loves you for a long, long time, not just to play with, but REALLY loves you, then you become Real."
> "Does it hurt?" asked the Rabbit.
> "Sometimes," said the Skin Horse, for he was always truthful. "When you are Real you don't mind being hurt."

"Does it happen all at once, like being wound up," he asked, "or bit by bit?"

"You become. It takes a long time. That's why it doesn't often happen to people who break easily, or have sharp edges, or who have to be carefully kept. Generally, by the time you are Real, most of your hair has been loved off, and your eyes drop out and you get loose in the joints and very shabby. But these things don't matter at all, because once you are Real you can't be ugly, except to people who don't understand."

"I suppose you are Real?" said the Rabbit. And then he wished he had not said it, for he thought the Skin Horse might be sensitive. But the Skin Horse only smiled.

"The Boy's Uncle made me Real," he said. "That was a great many years ago; but once you are Real you can't become unreal again. It lasts for always."

As the Velveteen Rabbit learned, the process of spiritual maturing and heart opening that is necessary for generativity takes strength and adaptability. It doesn't happen to everybody. It happens through love and intimate relationships—and giving is its essence.

CHAPTER NINE

Life: A Generous Giver

Everything is gestation and then bringing forth. To let each impression and each germ of a feeling come to completion wholly in itself, in the dark, in the inexpressible, the unconscious, beyond the reach of one's own intelligence, and await with deep humility and patience the birth-hour of a new clarity: that alone is living the artist's life: in understanding as in creating.

—RAINER MARIA RILKE

I F WE CHOOSE TO LIVE WELL, to gain the rewards of maturing generativity, we need to give birth to new ways of thinking and living, to new values in the second half of life. We can trust that the life we need to live is imprinted deep within us. Our main task is to let go of that which will block the birth. G. Spencer Brown, a British mathematician, wrote of this in his book *Laws of Form*. He knew the power of the inner life and its gestation, the power of taking time to allow something new to be born. To arrive at the simplest truth, Brown acknowledged, requires years of contemplation.

Brown could find little guidance for the kind of gestation time he needed. He found the process did not include reasoning, talking, reading, calculating, acting, or thinking.

131

He learned to simply bear in mind what it was he needed to know. In order to claim such quality of time, he had to pretend to be actively and diligently engaged in "work." Learning to claim the reflective time we need is important if we are going to give birth to a new way and live lives rich with meaning.

Many of the ideals and goals which served us well in the first half of life fall before the challenges of the second half. Those who change in accordance with the deeper design of life will reap benefits for themselves and those around them. Those who hold on to the inadequate goals of youth will increasingly become disheartened until life and aging brings, in Erikson's words, despair and disgust.

In youth, we are required to take the outer life and its demands seriously. Our creativity turns out to others, to expressing ourselves in the world, to acquiring survival skills, training, and education. We devote time and energy to earning a living and learn how to be a useful human being and citizen. We learn what our culture requires of us and how to meet those requirements as best we can. Young adulthood is also the time to form intimate relationships, and a time for bearing and rearing children.

After these tasks are entered into and mastered to some degree, a transition time beckons—middle adulthood. During this time, we face that some of our youthful hopes will not be realized and perhaps our job horizons narrow. Our youthful attractiveness is changing and we don't know if we like the changes. We begin to feel our losses and look back on opportunities missed. The stresses of job, parents, and children are taking their toll. We feel our hormone levels dropping and fear our sexual abilities may diminish. It is a rocky time. One moment we are certain of our good looks and physical prowess, and the next we despair as we look in the mirror (especially in fluorescent lighting) and see a drained and wrinkling person gazing back at us.

Midlife is the time to begin to put together a new self-image. Questions of meaning and purpose assail us: What is in me now and where is my path? Will I have the determination and energy to make my path a reality? Who can mentor me? Why am I so afraid? Sometimes I just do not want to think about it, I want to pretend it won't happen to me—getting old. Yes, it happened to mother and dad but not to me.

All Is Not Possible

When we are young everything seems possible. We have energy, enthusiasm, dreams, and plans for the future. It is the time to push life's limits and "go for it." Sooner or later out of life's vast potential, we must come to the point of choosing particular persons or jobs or places to live. It begins to dawn on us that if we choose to be married, we miss out on all those other possible mates; if we take this job, we will lose all those other jobs we might consider. If we live in the city, we have to give up the country. If we live in the States, we give up France or Mexico.

We must make choices and experience the loss of options if we are to mature well in adulthood. People who avoid choosing and float along on possibilities—trying to avoid the pain of making mistakes—are committing a big error in judgment. In their fear of the future and of the tasks of adult life they are refusing to live fully. Victor Hugo in *Les Miserables* described what happens to those who fear the future. It is not the future they condemn with their fears, but themselves. The only way out of the future, Hugo said, is to die.

If we reach age fifty-two, seventy-one, or eighty-six some-day, what will those days really be like? What can we do now to ensure the quality of life we truly want?

A wise teacher, Sufi Bayazid, reviewed his life and offered us the truth toward which he evolved as he matured.

> I was a revolutionary when I was young and all my prayer to God was "Lord, give me the energy to change the world."
>
> As I approached middle age and realized that half my life was gone without my changing a single soul, I changed my prayer to "Lord, give me the grace to change all those who come in contact with me. Just my family and friends, and I shall be satisfied."
>
> Now that I am an old man and my days are numbered, my one prayer is, "Lord, give me the grace to change myself." If I had prayed for this right from the start I should not have wasted my life.

Those of us in midlife may find ourselves in the same place as Sufi Bayazid. We are looking at the circumstances of our lives and wishing things were different. For example, perhaps our intimate relationships are not meeting some of our needs for excitement, nourishment, and understanding.

Ben, a man in his fifties, experienced a growing discontent with his marriage. He and his wife seemed to be rubbing each other the wrong way and piling up grievances. Perhaps you can identify with Ben's experience of dissatisfaction.

What Is Marriage Really For?

What is marriage for, Ben wondered as he jogged along the lakeshore. He used this private time for reflection as well as exercise, finding that important insights came to him easily as he ran. He guided his footfalls along the wet edges where water caresses sand.

Right now he thought about Joan. They had shared much together over the years, but it seemed now that they shared less and less. As his feet beat their steady rhythm on the sand, he remembered an incident from the day before. It had left him with a nagging sense of failure.

Joan, a lawyer, had burst into their apartment after a session in court where she was representing her side of the Brower vs Brower case. "Ben!" she shouted, "I think I've found the missing piece in the case, I'm so pleased. . . . Ben, are you there?"

He had been deep in thought at the time. As a writer, he sought solitude so the inner world would reveal itself. Ben believed that this undervalued, subtle, inner world was slowly being lost, and he yearned to bring forward the ancient symbols and teachings. Joan's outburst shattered the scene he had been trying to create. He sighed and answered, "I'm up here, Joan, in my study."

Breathlessly Joan clambered up the stairs and flung open the door to his study. "Ben, let's celebrate! I think I've found the missing piece in the Brower case. I want to tell you all about it. Let's see if the Warrens can join us. I want to go to a place with music and dancing! I'm ready for a party. What do you say?"

"Ummm," Ben stalled. There was no way he wanted a loud celebration, and the Warrens couldn't talk about anything deeper than their gall bladders or the best bargain in town. What he was really hungry for was intimacy, a communion of thoughts, conversation, and a bottle of wine shared.

"I'd like to go out with you, Joan, but how about a quiet place? It's been a while since you and I have talked, I mean really talked. I miss you. Let's us have a date tonight."

Joan had been disappointed. The clash between their styles and personalities seemed to be happening more frequently. Joan's differentness had once intrigued Ben, but lately he felt abused by her often chaotic style. A sense of poverty at the core of their relationship haunted him.

Not that he wasn't grateful for her gifts. She could relate well to their teen-age children, sometimes better than he could. She liked their sports, friends, and numerous phone calls. Yet, something was missing. He yearned to share ideas, silence, even meditate with Joan. But she seemed uncomfortable with silence.

As he continued running along the lakeshore, his mind left all musings and entered another realm. He was aware of nothing; his steady foot falls, the early dawn colors, the fresh breeze off the lake, all faded into a timeless state, into a place that was more like home.

Ben returned to an awareness of the beauty of life all around him. His perceptions seemed clearer. He headed homeward, his churning thoughts more peaceful. He felt his love for Joan, but realized that part of him was also afraid. What he yearned for was a deeper communion—he felt so lonely sometimes. What is marriage really for? Am I expecting the impossible? Is there more to this relationship struggle than I am understanding? Ben wondered.

A Matter of the Heart

I spoke with Ben several months later. He and Joan had acknowledged their problem and had gone to a mediation specialist. Both had begun to work on some of the anger that had developed between them and was eroding their relationship. They developed a plan based on reflection and a solid understanding of the difficulties between them.

Acknowledging that intimacy was a major challenge in their lives, they agreed to move forward in the relationship. Having invested their lives in each other, they decided to work hard for their future. They also felt a commitment to something beyond their marriage and that the purpose of their relationship transcended the needs of just the two of them. There were children to be considered, but more than that, they felt an overreaching sense of love.

Ben began to speak out clearly for what he wanted instead of giving in to Joan's more assertive ways. His anger subsided as he accepted responsibility for seeing that his needs were recognized, negotiated, and met. Joan also took responsibility for managing her own social needs and did not expect Ben to fulfill all of them. It was hard work at first as they struggled to make the changes, but Ben felt it was worth it. In fact he felt surprised at the new ways he is appreciating Joan these days.

Musings and questionings like Ben's come to all of us, especially in our middle years, as we consider some of the irksome characteristics of the people in our important relationships. This is the time we ask ourselves what it means to live with our early choices. Were they really the best ones for us? Many of us wonder if we have the energy to change some of these choices or whether it would be best simply to accept what we have. "When is it creative to adapt?" "When is it creative to change?"

Some of the reasons people decide to get together are for companionship, economic security, and sexual fulfillment. These reasons, however, are not enough for fulfillment because our needs are deeper than these somewhat superficial motivations. What really satisfies us is to enter the territory of the heart, acknowledging that loving and living from the heart is our highest calling.

Heart living includes, and extends beyond, primary relationships. To have perspective on the condition of your heart now, scan your life and ask yourself, Am I living my life from a full heart or do I see areas where I am half-hearted, doing things I don't like with a begrudging, miserly attitude? Am I living from an open, accessible heart or are there areas where I am closed, guarded, and don't want to let anybody in? Am I living from a whole heart, whole-heartedly embracing life or is my heart broken, hurt, disunited?

Recognizing the walls around our hearts that isolate us from others and seeing the ways we have walled in and walled out is essential to our well-being. We may ask ourselves, "Am I ready to experience what may be on the other side of my wall?" This is a spiritual quest.

Our relationships are more than they seem. What could love's purpose be? Is it freedom? Safety? Romance? Is there a mystical sense of purpose that is beyond the personal wants of the people involved? I believe so.

Spiritual intimacy is a powerful foundation for any relationship. Many of us are beginning to sense that our intimate relationships can be much more than we've understood so far. When we dare the journey into the sweet territory of the heart we release a healing balm, an elixir that turns life to pure gold. Long-term relationships between people who are willing to grow and develop release love and healing into the world. Just being in the presence of people who know how to love is transformative.

Whitehead and Whitehead in their work on adult development gave us a warning. They noted that failure in adult growth appears to be more related to remaining uncommitted (to particular persons, places, and jobs), than to problems inherent in commitment. Problems and limitations naturally crop up when we commit to a spouse, friend, or particular job. But avoiding the frustrations inherent in sustained commitments blocks our ability to express creativity and generativity.

We live in a world that values instant gratification, effortless relating, romantic idealism. Committing ourselves to loving another over many years is a brave and soul-shaping task. Seeing committed relationship as a path to wise maturity is a newer way to look at love. By engaging in the basic commitment to keep growing and keep opening the heart, all differences can be reconciled. When we take seriously the challenge of long-term love, we avoid the shattering of lives and hearts that often results from breakups.

Friends as Recruited Family

A primary task in the second half of life is to find and deepen relationships. We cannot mature in generativity unless we practice the lessons of intimacy. Usually we think of family as a unit of people bound by a blood relationship, but we can create other forms of family; deep friendship can enrich our lives. There are different levels of friendship. Some move from the usual superficial pleasantries to sacred ground and we become bonded in a secure and committed way. We naturally take on responsibility for our friends' lives and they return that to us. Friends help heal the hurts of life and fill in some of the deficits where other relationships have proved inadequate for our needs. We dare to be more than we know ourselves to be within the safe space provided by a warm and affirmative friend.

One problem with the elderly is that often they are not loved or listened to because many of their friends are gone and they did not make new ones. A witty, wise old woman faced this head on. Taking steps to retain a rich and enjoyable life, she cultivated new friends from the younger generations. "They'll outlast me!" she said with a chuckle. One of her strategies in this endeavor is to make sure she is not bored or boring!

Friends can fill our needs for a caring family. People may be separated from their birth families because of physical or emotional distance. Planning celebrations with "chosen" families can replace absent or incompatible relatives at holidays and special festivities. For instance, one family I know adopted an honorary grandmother twenty-three years ago. Through the years, she shared in family celebrations, bringing and receiving presents, helping and being helped when crises developed. Everyone has been enriched. It can be easier to be friends with a chosen family—there is no historical guilt or "shoulds" as there often is with one's parents or adult children.

My husband and I have chosen several young people to be part of our family life, often including them on family trips and celebrations. One unusual year we had nine children in college (our own plus others), supporting them emotionally and financially as needed. These are young people who otherwise may have felt abandoned, with unmet needs. We receive so much from them—our relationship is reciprocal.

Friends as Supports

In addition, we have good times with four other people in our age group. Once every four to six weeks, we gather at each other's homes for an overnight time together. We have been drawn into each other's family systems—encouraging and supporting young adult children, reassuring aging parents.

Those who embark on the way of maturing generativity may face the problem of friendships that no longer work. When one person moves on developmentally and the other does not, things often become strained and misunderstandings develop. Sometimes we find we need to change some of our friends as we change, which can be difficult. We need the support of a community of people who are also choosing generativity.

Making good friends takes a bit of self-confidence. We need a sense that we have something to offer, that the other would enjoy us. When David and I were married we both came to the relationship with a different set of friends. It became important to find "our" friends, and we began a series of small dinner parties for those who were likely potential friends for both of us. One of those parties brought the group of six of us together—the dear people mentioned earlier. I was the only one who knew everyone, but there was immediate chemistry between us all. And it has lasted. But what if I hadn't taken the lead and looked for friends? We might have missed this most rewarding human connection!

Keep in mind that we are talking about intimate, trusting long-term relationships. There is a difference between acquaintances and friends. Acquaintances meet our business and social needs and may become friends, but the friendship of which I speak is far deeper. In deciding to initiate an acquaintance that may lead to friendship, we need to have enough self-confidence to recover if we are rebuffed. In reaching out to others, we need courage and the ability to take risks.

It is best to cultivate several friends for our diverse needs. Some people can meet our desires to celebrate; others are good comforters and have a deep capacity to help us weather emotional storms. Some are wiser, some more

141

knowledgeable. Friends can help each other in practical ways, and helping one another creates strong bonds. Friendship often includes hugging and touching. As we age, we need the loving touch—especially if we do not have mates. Our craving for intimacy can be met in deep friendships.

One woman speaks of her inanimate friends like good books, her computer, her bicycle. She also cultivates herself as a friend, enjoying her own company. Pets can fill in some lonely places. Even a bird feeder that attracts beautiful feathered friends can be a source of pleasure and heart-warmth.

Be creative in initiating and fostering your friendships. A small group of men I know meets every few weeks in each other's homes. The host provides the dinner for the evening and they talk about everything that is on their minds: business, aging, sexuality, world situations, mates, health, fears, problems, money, and more. They consider cooking the meal a very important part of the evening and complain if the host has ordered Chinese carry-out too often!

Relationships provide the fastest and clearest way to see shadow parts of ourselves that have been denied or buried. We have to embrace our basic flaws and negative feelings for true intimacy to grow. We can be intimate and openhearted to others only if we are intimate and openhearted to ourselves.

The solution to our deepest problems in relationship is *within the problem* itself. Often we try to run away from problems only to recreate them again in different settings and with different players on the stage of our lives. In grappling with the problem itself we will reap the desired harvest of love and compassionate caring. Friends are like mirrors to more clearly see who we are—the shadow and the light. Recently I had such a mirror experience and felt compelled to write a poem celebrating it.

MIRRORS

In my old file cabinet
way in the back
a dusty folder
caught my eye
"Letters To Keep"

I read
and time reversed.
With forgotten passion
—and presence
people rose
from memory's grave.

An earlier me
rose too,
enlivened in the words.

For a letter
is a bridge.
No, two bridges
spanning time
and people.

Who were we then?
Who was I?
Somehow, I forgot.

But there I was
the me of so long ago
reflected back

and I respected my earlier self
today,
because of them,
—more than
yesterday.

143

Responsibility

Responsibility is a very freeing attitude. When I endure the pain of seeing how I have helped create my own problems and how often I have refused the liberating step life has offered me—not just once but many times—I begin to see that I have the power to choose a different lifestyle. Responsibility is the beginning of freedom and the golden doorway to increased happiness and fulfillment.

It is a liberating step to accept responsibility for the way our lives are turning out. Response-ability means that I have power to move and change my life by responding to the elements in it with creativity, informed by clarity, wisdom, and perseverance.

I have known Hallie for years. She is so talented, attractive, and bright that I would love to have her for a good friend—except that she plays the victim role, blaming others for her problems and her hardships. A widow in her fifties, Hallie's life becomes more dreary each year and her problems seem to grow as though they have a life of their own. People avoid her because they feel drained by her negative attitudes and thoughts. Her daughters and sons feel loyalty and responsibility toward her, yet they also see how she sabotages herself and her life and then wants someone to rescue her. Over the years they have gradually moved away from her emotionally and physically.

Hallie is refusing to carry her own life with responsibility. It wasn't so noticeable when she was younger, but becomes increasingly clear as she ages and choice leads to choice. Opportunities have often come to Hallie—forks in the road of her life. She has refused the new and has clung to her belief that life is terrible and she is a helpless victim. By blaming life and others, by spending time with those who perceive things as she does, she avoids the humbling work of seeing her part in her problems.

Accepting the responsibility for our lives appears to open the door to the gifts of life as well as the hard times. William chose to accept the responsibility of his life.

Will is in his late forties. He remembered a time when things were very hard for him, a time when he felt vaguely uneasy and his vitality was gone. He had a responsible job in the family business, but he could hardly make himself get up and go to work. Will was also concerned about his weight; gradually he had put on forty-five extra pounds. He had tried diets, but the weight just came back on.

His father's illness weighed on his mind, too; everyone knew his condition was terminal. Will had two children in college and a stable marriage, but his wife kept nagging him about his weight, and he knew she found him less appealing sexually.

A friend invited Will to a noon meeting of Overeaters Anonymous (OA), a group of people who use a twelve-step program to explore their shared concern about poor eating patterns. He assured Will that he didn't have to do or say anything, just observe. Will was feeling desperate about so many areas of his life and wondered what good one meeting would do, but he decided to try it anyway.

Will expected to see a room of obese people and was surprised to be with people who were clearly recovering. This was the beginning for Will, a slow process of getting to know who he was and why he used food inappropriately. He learned to listen to the voice behind the hunger—the voice that wanted to tell him the truth about himself.

In the weeks that followed, Will began to piece together his life story. From early on, he was trained to take over the family business. "Will, we have worked hard to make this

145

family business a success. It's a gold mine; it will be a good life." Will, however, never found his own personal dream.

Will realized that he had given away his power to his family to determine the direction of his life. He had also accepted their value that money was the most important thing. Will finally realized he had a choice, that he had the power to do things differently, something he had not really thought about before.

As Will began taking responsibility for his life and his choices, he found he could stop eating between meals so much. He continued going to OA, for by now he loved the people there—they gave him the strength and support to face his life. He began making important changes.

He kept the family business, not because of the ghosts of his father and grandfather, but because it provided freedom for his other interests. Will now gives career counseling workshops in the high school and often takes young people under his wing. Because he accepted responsibility in mid-life for the truth of his life, he gave himself permission to shape and direct it in the path that was right for him. He recognized that his problems were really disguised gifts from the generous giver—Life.

Freely Offered Gifts

In 1513, a wise person named Fra Giovanni wrote of the gifts that are around us at all times. Giovanni counseled a distressed loved one to take the freely offered gifts:

> I am your friend and my love for you goes deep. There is nothing I can give you which you have not got: but there is much, very much that, while I cannot give it, you can take.

146

No heaven can come to us unless our hearts find rest in today. TAKE HEAVEN! No peace lies in the future which is not hidden in this present little instant. TAKE PEACE!

The gloom of the world is but a shadow. Behind it yet within our reach is JOY! There is radiance and glory in the darkness, could we but see—and to see we have only to look. I BESEECH YOU TO LOOK!

Life is so generous a giver, but we, judging its gifts by their covering, cast them away as ugly or heavy or hard. Remove the covering and you will find beneath it a living splendour, woven of love, by wisdom, with power.

Welcome it, grasp it, and you touch the Angel's hand that brings it to you. Everything we call a trial, a sorrow, or a duty, believe me that Angel's hand is there; the gift is there, and the wonder of an overshadowing Presence. Our joys too. Be not content with them as joys. They, too, conceal diviner gifts.

And so at this time I greet you, not quite as the world sends greetings, but with profound esteem and the prayer that for you, NOW AND FOREVER, the day breaks and shadows flee away.

Whether or not we do the work of facing the realities of our lives, humbly accepting the inherent gifts, life keeps moving us along. At the very root of our lives is the time factor. When we accept this, we can form a partnership with time, reaping the rewards that are ours in the second half of life.

Good? Bad? Who Knows?

Some of the negative images of aging we currently have are the result of not realizing or living out the advantages of the second half of life. By default we in the later years have given away our power to the peddlers of youth.

In a way, many of us have earned this indictment. With a few noteworthy exceptions, most of us fade off, giving away our wisdom and power possibilities. I was speaking of this at a conference on aging recently. A man came up after my talk and told of visiting Phoenix, Arizona. He and his wife became depressed watching the "retired" population, still physically healthy and so able to be useful. They passed their days playing golf and partying without ceasing. Even as I write this, some of you may be saying, "Yes, that's exactly what I want . . ." However, continual playing without significance will turn sour. As one of the men in the study found for himself, "How long can you just play golf and still respect yourself?" he asked.

To age well, to live well, is to see life as an adventure, to stand against the cultural prejudice about growing old and affirm that "being" is as valuable as "doing." It means to creatively accept the infirmities which come as the body wears out and maintain a spirit that grows healthier, wiser. We calmly set about to do what we can, knowing that all is essentially well, even if at the moment there might be some difficulties. An old Chinese story illustrates this wisdom.

A wise old farmer had a useful work horse to help him till his fields. One day the horse broke loose and ran away. The people of the village sympathized with the old farmer over his bad luck. The farmer's reply was "Bad luck? Good luck? Who knows?"

A few days later, the horse returned with eight other horses. This time the villagers congratulated him for his good luck. The old farmer replied "Good luck? Bad luck? Who knows?"

The farmer's son was riding one of the unfamiliar horses when it reared and he fell and broke his leg. The villagers all thought this was very bad, but not the farmer. Again, he kept his cool saying "Bad luck? Good luck? Who knows?"

A month later soldiers marched through the little village conscripting all the healthy young men. However, when they saw the farmer's son in bed with his broken leg, they went on. The farmer kept his equilibrium—"Good luck? Bad luck? Who knows?"

That which seems hard, "bad luck" on the surface, can be a hidden blessing on the path of generativity. We judge life's gifts by their covering and cast them away as ugly, heavy, or hard, missing the love and wisdom which those gifts contain. Life is a generous giver—let's not throw those gifts away unopened.

CHAPTER TEN

Family Dynamics
and Our True Self

Open my eyes, that I may see
Glimpses of truth Thou hast for me
Place in my hands the wonderful key
That shall unclasp and set me free.
Silently now I wait for Thee
Ready, my God, Thy will to see;
Open my eyes, illumine me, Spirit Divine.

—OLD HYMN

M OST OF US WHO ARE PARENTS and have arrived in our forties and fifties have begun to recognize the mistakes and inadequacies of our parenting skills while we were raising our children, even though we tried to do the best we could. Often we feel pained when we become aware of how we have passed along family problems. In my younger years I vowed I would handle life and children very differently than did my parents. Have some of you felt that too? We were naive and did not understand the pressures that would come to us later. We were unaware of the predictable human tendencies to repeat with others—especially children—what was done to us.

151

Scratch the surface of almost any family system and you will see the destructive adaptations to repressed traumas. We are in an emergency situation in our culture—the family is in deep trouble.

I attended a conference recently where a panel of scientists and psychologists were in dialogue with the Dalai Lama. The question was asked, "We notice that there is less family violence in Tibet than in our country. Could you tell us why?"

The Dalai Lama said it was hard to come up with an answer because no one investigates these things. But when an episode of family violence happens in Tibet people are surprised because it is so unusual.

The Dalai Lama asked the U.S. panel members why child abuse is increasing here. The panel observed that we in the U.S. see violence a lot—we give permission for violent acts through constant depictions on TV, in films, in newspapers and magazines. Guns are also easily available and desperate people, often under the influence of alcohol and other substances, frequently choose violent responses to their relationship problems.

After observing our culture and our television programming the Dalai Lama spoke about the strong daily emphasis on sex, violence, and money. The public likes to be aroused, he noted, and the media and public must mutually share the responsibility for this destructive emphasis. He suggested that to reduce abuse in families, we should design educational strategies and present them through the media. He encouraged us to introduce the need for compassion as basic to the development of the full human being. He challenged us to awaken the younger generations so they will understand that developing compassion is essential in today's world, that it is not religious to be compassionate but

152

practical—our survival depends on it. The family is the core unit of society, and if the family heals, this compassionate flow will spread outward, healing the larger community.

Compassion Is Needed

It seems that a challenge fitting for the rich years of life after forty is the cultivation of compassion, which leads to compassionate action. It begins in our own hearts, then spreads to our families and to others. Compassion is an energy long associated with the feminine principle. Certainly it is not news that the feminine component of life has been distorted and undermined, not only in our own culture but worldwide.

Powerful masculine energy dominates the times we live in, and the resulting imbalance is destructive. Riane Eisler's book, *The Chalice and the Blade,* documents archaeological examples of cultures which existed some 3,000 to 8,000 years ago that had an egalitarian balance between masculine and feminine values. She named them "partnership societies."

The qualities associated with the feminine end of the masculine/feminine polarity are nurturing, caretaking, connecting, and containing—just the qualities needed to foster new life. The masculine qualities of assertive action, useful for protecting new life, form the counter-balance. (I am referring to a range of values and characteristics associated with the feminine and masculine principles. Individuals of both sexes have greater or lesser degrees of the whole range of qualities.) Because feminine values have been unpopular and women have (until recently) lacked the assertive self-esteem they needed, qualities like compassion, essential for healthy human interaction, have been subjugated and sabotaged.

153

Our missing relational skills and family breakdowns are hurting everyone. Consider the newspaper story of a ninth-grade boy with family problems who came to school armed with a shotgun and a pistol, taking a class hostage. When the police came he stated his terms: he wanted to see his father who had remarried and had another family. He threatened that he would begin to shoot if he couldn't have communication with his dad. This boy–crying out for relationship, for his birthright, an understanding father to be with and to learn from—highlights our crisis of family.

The Marriage of Masculine and Feminine

Perhaps, however, different kinds of family dynamics are emerging. Small groups of people are participating in discussions on how to initiate and cultivate true manhood, true womanhood. They are interested in growing toward right relationship with the feminine side of life.

Developed men are recognizing their sage potential, learning to handle power in psychological, mental, spiritual, and physical realms. They are embracing the lover quality in themselves, able to connect emotionally on all levels. Mature women are cultivating healthy self-esteem leading to assertive action on behalf of their values. Individuals are honoring their opposites, and men and women, the halves of the whole, are perhaps becoming truly reconciled.

When the great marriage of the masculine and feminine polarities takes place, everyone benefits; vitality comes, joy based on strength from within emerges, vision clears. We begin to feel at ease and playful, and we gain a deep sense that life is good.

154

Courage to Change Patterns
in Intimate Relationships

Midlife is a fertile time to do the work of relating well with one another and gain a clearer understanding of our difficulties. We can start to learn from the people we are deeply connected with through birth or choice—our families. I use the word "family" to include the new forms of family we are creating through choice—blended families from second or third marriages, friends included as honorary relatives, close, committed, and enduring relationships of many kinds.

Families have characteristic behavior patterns that have developed over time and are often rigidly in place. Frequently the people in the family system have taken on roles handed down for several generations. People also attract and marry those who fit the generational patterns and roles. Changing these entrenched attitudes and behaviors requires considerable skill and strength.

Harriet Lerner in her book, *The Dance of Anger,* described the predictable process in a family system when one member wants to initiate change: (1) the old in-place pattern exists, (2) someone in the family introduces a new behavior, (3) opposition or countermoves are taken by other family members. Some common countermoves Lerner has observed include accusing the one introducing the change of coldness, disloyalty, selfishness, or disregard for others. Other countermoves can take the form of an accident, asthma attack, or stroke suffered by family members. If people refuse to initiate needed change they sacrifice themselves to the existing pattern, and "de-self" themselves—gaining a painful legacy of anger and blame instead.

A Countermove: Gregg's Story

A young friend of mine, Gregg, told me of his mother's experience with a countermove. A woman in her late fifties with a concern for the rain forests, his mother had decided to join a fact-finding trip to the rain forests in the Amazon basin. From the beginning her husband was against it. He stated many reasons why: it was too expensive, she might get sick in a Third World country, she might get hurt, she was getting too old for this kind of travel, and so on. She would reassure him, but continued with her plans. He became more threatening, warning her of dire results if she continued on her course. She wavered some, but her friends supported her decision to go.

One week before the departure date, her husband fell and broke his leg. He needed surgery and would be incapacitated for weeks. She cancelled her trip, but she felt angry and sabotaged.

A year later, Gregg was at a family reunion and overheard his mother speaking of her cancelled trip. His father chimed in with a joke saying "Yeah, I broke my leg so she couldn't go." Everyone but Gregg and his mother laughed. After all, accidents happen.

But was it really an accident, or was something more complex going on? Gregg's father had put himself in quite a state of anxiety over his wife's trip and had tried many strategies to dissuade her. At some level he seemed to be getting increasingly desperate about the trip.

Harriet Lerner's research supports the notion that we can bring sickness and other incidents on ourselves in a countermove to try to control someone close to us. In all families there can be powerful opposition to one person initiating a more separate position. The opposition will accuse the one

156

changing of being wrong and ask the changing person to go back to the old ways. If this doesn't work, they will begin to use threats.

New Moves in My Family System

In my life, as I become increasingly true to myself, I started making new moves in my family. Here is an example.

Often my side of the family gathers for a couple days over Labor Day weekend—sometimes twenty to twenty-five people ages one to sixty-four years. I really love my family and David does, too, and we have always hosted these events. Others bring food and pitch in, but I have always felt compelled to bear the brunt of the responsibility.

One summer as Labor Day neared, I realized that I had a knot in my stomach; a reunion at our house was not right for me this year. I felt guilty and selfish, but there it was. David wanted the reunion, so we had some negotiating to do. Finally I came to a compromise: it was fine for everyone to be at our house, but it was not fine for me to be there.

David was a little jarred at first, but after a bit he could accept my position. I wrote everyone a letter expressing my feelings and sent it off:

Dear Family,

I am writing this because I will not be seeing you over Labor Day. Although I will not be here, I know David will serve as a good host.

I want to explain about my absence during your reunion. Very early in life I got the message that I was to "take care of" people. I am now re-writing this script.

Because of my personal saga, I cannot be present at a

big family gathering—I am just a bit vulnerable right now. Having it at my house triggers all those old tapes that tell me I am supposed to make everything all right for every- body. Until I become healthier (and I know that will hap- pen) and can do things in a different way, I need to do some things that will support my evolving future and will help me release more of the past and its restraints.

Please accept my apologies and this explanation. I apologize only that I am not free to join you, but not for finding ways to meet my needs and continue on my path of growth. As each of us in this family grows and changes, I hope that we can adapt, accept, and encourage each other to become as unique as God—who didn't even make two snowflakes alike—intended us to become.

I hope you have a really wonderful time!

Love, Paula

Expect Unexpected Affirmations on the Way

Changing the old parental attitudes that have become life scripts for us requires hard work, courage, and persistence. Often the new approach will feel wrong, even selfish. Oth- ers may not like the changes and may try to make us feel guilty. The old behaviors feel "right" in some way, so moving from what seems familiar and secure to what feels selfish and strange can bring anxiety. But be assured that such anxiety is really a sign of progress. Often you will find unex- pected reinforcement for your changes from unexpected sources. This surprising approval can come from anyone, anywhere, as I learned for myself.

When I made my decision not to attend the reunion, I won- dered what to do with my free weekend. Then I remembered how much I had been wanting to visit San Francisco. In spite of feeling selfish, I called a travel agent and explained that I was just exploring prices. I had a knot in my stomach—what if the ticket cost $450 or $500; could I justify doing it?

The agent said there was a special round trip fare on American Airlines for $152. Neither of us could believe it! She checked her computer again—yes, $152. I felt my decision had been affirmed!

Several days later I had occasion to call the same agent. "You know," she said, "the fare you got was in the computer only briefly. It turns out there was a computer error at American Airlines and some people got these very low fares before they could correct it. The fates must have really wanted you to go!"

I had a marvelous trip and the family had a great reunion, but I felt there were some unresolved strains in my relationships with my siblings. It is a process that will take time.

Over a year passed and it was Thanksgiving. By now the family was beginning to adjust to my new behaviors, and several of the younger generation decided to take charge of a family reunion. One nephew was on the board of an organization that was rehabilitating a hunting lodge, and he made arrangements for us to use it without charge if we cleaned up afterwards. It was so much better! Because I stepped down, it empowered the young people, encouraging their initiative.

This illustrates a spiritual law I see affirmed over and over. When you do what is *really* right for your true Self, it is *really* right for everyone else. Even if it feels selfish at first, even if people do not understand, even if you feel afraid, it will turn out well in the long run. Try that one out and let me know if it works for you!

Attempted Repair Work: A Father's Story

One father, now in his early sixties, chose to learn better caring skills. He has been working at this process for about seven or eight years. He began by realizing that something was amiss in his life and started a program of therapy and self-reflection to fill in what was missing. As he changed, he wanted to reach out to his grown children in a new way. One of his strategies was to invite them individually to a function or event that would interest them.

Two years ago he chose to invite a daughter from whom he felt estranged on a father-daughter trip to Stratford in Canada. With their permission, I share a journal-like story he wrote of the event, which he sent to his daughter.

A TRIP TO STRATFORD

She picked him up at the Detroit airport. They were both anticipating the summer outing with a mixture of enthusiasm and apprehension. Eager to begin to build a new relationship with his twenty-eight-year-old daughter, he wanted to offer a connection that could have warmth and meaning. Things were strained from a history that hadn't been particularly healthy for her.

He had come to know that their family had been dysfunctional from the start of his wife's lengthy illness, maybe well before that. He had a sense that his daughters had seen him as demanding things which could not be given. Now the time seemed right to say goodbye to some of that.

The children had been hostages to the events around the illness and death. A succession of nurses, some kind, some not, had controlled the household. Both parents had not been very good listeners, and the little girls weren't able to articulate their pain.

He felt his daughter's judgment about their history was sometimes a harsh judgment, or so it seemed to him. He was resolved to seek a closer, more rewarding father-daughter relationship.

His daughter looked lovely and seemed glad to see him. They were both looking forward to the plays to be seen at the Stratford Festival across the river. It would be a three-hour drive. For his part, he hoped to enjoy the Shakespeare plays, dramas that had often eluded him. She loved and understood Shakespeare.

She had come well prepared, and on the way up in the car she gave him a thorough briefing on the plays, along with fresh peaches and orange juice. The trip went quickly. Both seemed determined that it should be pleasant, and it was. They arrived at their hotel, an inn with a pub and dining room—very British.

The trip surfaced some ambiguous issues for him. What is a healthy role for the father of a young woman? A friend? A mentor? A parent? What responsibilities belong to him? He could see where she struggled, yet he often failed to see his own impact on these struggles.

That evening they ate with a young man friend of his daughter's. He sensed that she was a little anxious about her father coming on too strong. He probably did.

Returning to Detroit she expressed some anger about their earlier lives again and yet he felt their relationship had basically changed for the better. He sensed a loneliness in her. She dropped him at the airport with a hug. He wondered when they would see each other again.

In this story, the father and daughter are struggling with a shared painful history, and yet each experienced that history very differently. Even though he now realizes some of his mistakes in the relationship, the father may want resolution too quickly. One wonders if he still is pressuring her to be different than she is, repeating his earlier mistake of "demanding things which could not be given"?

In the second half of life we need much patience with those who are younger and perhaps do not see as yet what we have learned to see. We need to respect that they have their own agendas. When the father says "Now the time seemed right to say goodbye to some of that," he is speaking from his point of view, but is he setting up a timetable for the daughter for which she is not ready?

Often when we break through to new understandings, we want other family members to do the same—the truth seems so obvious now. For lasting and fruitful change to occur, however, it is important to allow the process to happen slowly. In our story, the father is understandably uncomfortable with his daughter's anger. Yet it exists for a reason and may serve a very important function for her. Perhaps the father's work now is to further develop a calm, nonblaming attitude toward his daughter's process. Within this safe environment, continued and lasting healing can occur for both of them.

Relationship, The Teacher of the Heart

Recently I met a woman in her late sixties who was wise in the ways of families. She gained her experience from her work as a therapist as well as from her own family situation. She gave me her five-year guideline. She noticed that young adult children who need to break away take about five years to go through the process of (1) recognizing some of the pain in their childhoods, (2) blaming the parent or parents, feeling angry, separating from them, being out of touch, then (3) beginning to initiate small moves toward reconnecting, and (4) developing a new pattern of relationship in which they and their parents become more like adult friends.

Essential to life from beginning to end are our connections to others. Yet what is called love can sometimes bind, distort, and sabotage human promise. We may swing between possessing and being possessed. Sometimes, thinking we know best, we try to live another's life. Perhaps we let another tell us what to do too many times and then find ourselves angry and impotent because we've diminished who we are.

Relationship is the great teacher of the heart. It comes in many forms and holds up many mirrors as we learn who we are. In discovering our true Self, separate and whole, we begin to exchange dependence for interdependence, and learn to create family relationships in new and healthier ways.

CHAPTER ELEVEN

The Child of Yesterday,
The Adult of Today

> Know the strength of man,
> But keep a woman's care!
> Become as a little child once more.
>
> —Lao Tsu

IN CHILDHOOD, WE REACTED TO OUR FEELINGS with authenticity and immediacy. We cried when we hurt, we "told it like it was." If someone had a gigantic nose, we would be openly intrigued. We were in touch with our bodies and got stomach aches when we felt sad. We were unashamedly sensuous. It may may take a long time to reclaim this spontaneous zesty quality of our childhood. If you haven't reclaimed the child within you it's time to do it now, because none of us can fulfill our promise without this resource.

In regaining our child, we do not sacrifice reason and mature judgment, but we do add spontaneity, playfulness, and wise innocence. We also gain a freedom from social conventions and cultural norms. These benefits come because we have struggled with self-centeredness and transcended this downward pull. If we have not done this inner work, we might fall into some of the negative qualities of unsuccessful aging like childishness, petulance, and meanness of spirit.

When we regain our child, we balance pragmatic wisdom with inspiration. Our life becomes wholly natural and we are sources of strength to those we touch. We enjoy our gift of emancipated, childlike innocence with its ready laughter and easy tears. This desirable state resembles what many religious traditions call enlightenment.

Poet Delmore Schwartz caught this light-hearted yet wise quality of the child:

I AM CHERRY ALIVE

"I am cherry alive," the little girl sang.
"Each morning I am something new:
I am apple, I am plum, I am just as excited
As the boys who made the Hallowe'en bang:
I am tree, I am cat, I am blossom too:
When I like, if I like, I can be someone new,
Someone very old, a witch in a zoo:
I can be someone else whenever I think who,
And the peach has a pit and I know that too,
And I put it in along with everything
To make the grown-ups laugh whenever I sing:
And I sing: it is true; it is untrue,
The peach has a pit,
The pit has a peach:
And both may be wrong
When I sing my song,
But I don't tell the grown-ups: because it is sad,
And I want them to laugh just like I do

166

Because they grew up
And forgot what they knew
And they are sure
I will forget it someday too.
They are wrong. They are wrong.
When I sang my song, I knew, I knew!
I am red,
I am gold,
I am green,
I am blue,
I will always be me,
I will always be new!"

Charles Whitfield, a physician who has studied the inner child in adults, defined the child within as our Real Self. It is that part of us that is totally alive, vital, creative, spontaneous, and fulfilled. Whitfield used capital letters when referring to this most valuable Inner Core. He explained that when the Child Within is not permitted to flourish and be its Real Self, a false or co-dependent self emerges that learns to adapt and take on the victim role. Whitfield presented some grim statistics: most of us came from homes that didn't allow the child to be its Real Self and instead fostered a contorted human formation through shaming, criticizing, and teasing. Our child's feelings and wants were minimized through belittling, discrediting, and withholding love.

Usually we have repressed a great deal about our childhood and our home environment. We want to be loyal to our families, and, at some level, we realize they did the best they could. Although it is true they did the best they could, nevertheless, our child was terribly hurt in the process.

Maybe we are a little afraid of uncovering some of those painful early feelings, so we compensate. We deny what is true and bury ourselves in work, alcohol, busy-ness, TV, sports, sex. We continue to "protect" our parents by avoiding our real feelings and the memories of conflict, pain, and anger.

By refusing to admit our feelings we pass a life prison sentence on ourselves. And, we pass on to our children the wounds we received, not because we want to, but because we know no other way. We also deny ourselves the healing love that can flow backward into the past and forward into the future.

Caring for the Next Generation

"Fellow citizens why do you turn and scrape every stone to gather wealth and take so little care of your children to whom someday you must relinquish all?" asked Socrates many years ago. The question of how we care for our children still faces us today, as Alice Miller demonstrates so convincingly in her book, *Thou Shalt Not Be Aware: Society's Betrayal of the Child.* Early childhood is of crucial importance for the development of emotional maturity necessary to care for others, she stated. Miller studied the roots of violence and human agony that originate in childhood. This damage to children done by families and social systems can have disastrous effects, which evidence themselves in subsequent destructive acts. The absurdity of ominous events going on in the world today, she said, have their origins in childhood trauma.

Miller's heritage is German and she studied the roots in her people's childhoods of the system that allowed the Holocaust to occur. Step by step her research depicted the typical German parental approach to children, which humiliated, shamed, and spanked them into an "obedient" people who could follow a person like Hitler with blind, uncompassionate, self-righteous loyalty.

We do not have to study pre-World War II Germany to find cultural child abuse. A special edition of *Newsweek* on children said that U.S. children were the most neglected in the developed world. I saw the effects of neglect and abuse during the two years I directed a grant for the U.S. Department of Health, Education and Welfare (now Health and Human Services) at Cook County Department of Corrections, a short-term detention facility. The purpose of the grant was to help young males gain employment upon release. I discovered from the testing they received that ninety percent had clearly been abused children. They explained their anti-social behaviors with such phrases as "I just went off, I don't know what happened, I just went off. . . ."

When adults are able to care in healthy ways, the well-being of others becomes a source of pleasure and fulfillment. Their personalities expand to take other people into their hearts. Identifying with others beyond one's self helps us to grow in scope and relevancy, and we find our personal happiness.

Because of the deep connection between maturing generativity and one's ability to care well for the next generation, I was interested to find that the men and women I studied were very involved with children. They were caring financially, emotionally, or in both ways for children of all kinds: biological, step, foster, extended family, adopted, grown, grandchildren, and other children. Thirteen people were caring for 112 children!

Ancient native American traditions are concerned with the children of the earth. Lynn Andrews, who apprenticed to a Cree medicine woman, passed their teachings along in her book *Flight of the Seventh Moon*. Andrews learned that the Crees and other tribes considered it a law of the universe to honor their children, to develop womblike caring qualities in all people, whether male or female. If this womb quality is dead, there is no understanding for children. Those who hurt children are those who do not honor their own child within.

Two thousand years ago, three New Testament authors recorded the story of Jesus rebuking his disciples for trying to prevent the little children from coming to him. Jesus used that event to teach: "Let the children come to me, do not hinder them; for to such belongs the kingdom of Heaven. Truly I say to you, whoever does not receive the kingdom of Heaven like a child shall not enter it."

What are the qualities of the little child, so valuable that we need to reclaim them in adulthood so we can partake of the state of bliss and delight that heaven symbolizes? What does this ancient wisdom say to us today?

Inner Child Wrestles with the Adult of Today

In middle adulthood the inner child long denied becomes increasingly insistent. It wants to be heard. Professionals who work with adults can often see the hidden inner child battling with the adult. Middle adulthood is the ripest time for coming to terms with our inner child and with the family secrets and history. It is a time to interview older members of the family system, to collect the stories and understand the forces that shaped the lives of our parents and grandparents.

We begin to see that we are part of a larger patchwork that, like a quilt, is sewn together into a pattern that makes sense and can be useful. We gain some idea of what has been passed to us and through us to others. We come to understand some of the forces our inner child had to contend with.

The inner child of yesterday is alive and wants to be free today. Carl Jung referred to this part of us as the Divine Child. In religious language the word "soul" is often used. All these terms attempt to describe our highest potential, which is connected to something greater.

When the connection to this most valuable resource is cleared and the fountain of Life bubbles up from deep within, we truly enter heaven. We pass through the golden door. Not only do we begin to taste the open-hearted transformative love for ourselves that heaven is all about, but we become a vehicle for others to begin to taste heaven as well.

Healing Comes in Many Ways

How do we begin to honor our little child within? There are many ways and it takes time. One expert said it takes three to five years to find and integrate the part of you symbolized by the child. My own healing continued with the nourishing example of a caring, attentive father on a train last year. I pass it on to you.

"AREN'T I BEAUTIFUL?"

Heading toward the big city on an almost empty, two-car train, I felt rested and refreshed. I had just spent a week at our beachside place, thinking, reading, and writing.

As the train gathered passengers at country stations along its route, a man in his thirties and a small girl of about four got on and seated themselves across the aisle from me. He was dressed in a crisp white shirt and gray-

171

on-gray textured slacks and carried a red Gore-tex bag with black handles. The child sported a comfortable-looking striped T-shirt dress with a pert red ribbon holding her ponytail in place.

I returned to the book I was reading until my eye was caught by a repetitive gesture. The father was shaking a bottle of nail polish, mixing the colors. Then he placed the red bag on his lap while she put five small fingers on the bag-table and watched as he painted her nails.

While her nails were drying, father pulled a storybook out of the red bag. She snuggled into the crook of his arm, holding her hands carefully so the nails wouldn't smudge.

"How much further, Daddy?"

"Ohhh, about an hour."

Storytime continued. I noticed the child got a little wiggly and forsook her niche in his arm. As she leaned forward, I got my first good look at her: sparkly brown eyes, clear pink cheeks, and sun-kissed summer skin. With her attention totally on daddy as he read, her face was like a responsive mirror, registering the story themes. I pondered how vulnerable and open she was to whatever he chose to read and say.

The book finished, she lay down on the seat beside him, her head on his lap. "That's a good idea. A rest will do you good," he encouraged her. His right hand cradled her head, his left lay protectively on her curled-up body.

The train neared the outskirts of the big city with its factories, pollution, shabby housing, abandoned autos, and scrubby trees here and there. Suddenly, I heard a harsh thump and the people around me shifted uneasily. Glancing up I saw an angry craze of cracks on the window by the little girl. Like a giant, Amazonian jungle spiderweb, the pattern of shattered glass glared back at me.

I saw the father shaking his head thoughtfully, slowly, releasing deep sighs, the child still asleep on his lap.

"Did you see it happen?" I asked him.

"Yes."

"What was it?"

"A rock—a young boy threw a rock at us."

"Ohhh," I responded, sobered.

"Chicago, Chicago next," came the announcement. The father roused the sleeping child and as she rubbed the dreams from her eyes, he placed the red bag on his lap again. I watched as he pulled from the magic bag a pair of fresh white socks with lace on them and a white pair of shoes. Slipping her sandals off, he covered the wiggling toes with their fresh garb. Next, he brought out a carefully folded white dress, all ruffly and endearing.

Then he stood her up on the seat. I saw his hand carefully pass over the web of cracks to make sure no splinters could harm her. He never mentioned a word about the incident and she, cheerfully unnoticing, turned her little face to look at the passing city outskirts through the cracks.

A hair brush and white ribbon came out of the red bag, and soon the transformation process was complete. As the train pulled into the station the child decided to make her move. Squeezing past daddy's knees, she stood in the aisle beside me. Looking right into my eyes and holding the skirt of her dress out with two small hands, she announced prettily, "Aren't I beautiful!"

Gaining Access to the Child Within

This story is an example of how love naturally blesses and nourishes the people around it. We can cultivate our own ability to recognize examples of love and enjoy them to our heart's content!

Life, ever the generous giver, provides many opportunities to gain access to the child within. We can trigger our awareness of our inner child's attitudes and needs through attentiveness, self-monitoring, and reflection strategies. If we pay attention to our dreams, they can give us vivid images of our inner landscape. As I kept on connecting to my inner child, I saw dream images of children—abused, crippled, starved, even dead. They triggered feelings in me that needed compassionate attention.

It may be important for some of you to get therapy to provide guidance, safety, and support. One woman began to feel the need to understand the sexual abuse in her childhood. She was uncomfortable around men and couldn't be assertive at work. Her boss would give her additional assignments and, although weary and stressed, she couldn't say no to a man. Her increasing exhaustion, anger, and feeling of being a victim of thoughtless people finally provided her with the impetus she needed to seek help.

There are many self-help groups available to us today. For example, the network of twelve-step programs all work with childhood influences. You can find their telephone numbers in your phone book. Reaching out for help enables us to transform the troublesome bonds of our lives into positive and empowering qualities.

Our healing process prompts us to pay attention to *all* our feelings and decide how to act on them most creatively. One day, I realized I wanted to go to a toy store and find a teddy bear. This may appear foolish to some—a woman in her fifties wanting a teddy bear, but it was my desire. I found a wonderful furry creature who called out to me from his deep-set brown eyes. I was so excited! A friend suggested the name Icon and that seemed just right. Since an icon is a religious symbol this seemed especially fitting for the reclaiming of my lost inner child, my true Self—a holy undertaking. I wrote this sonnet of my experience:

IN PRAISE OF TEDDY BEARS

A lithesome child I knew, though not so well,
A lovely child as pictured in my mind,
She disappeared one day, or so they tell—
Time passed along but no one searched to find.
A teddy bear all soft with listening ears
Told me a secret which the girl told it.
If I could hug a bear and face my fears
If I could laugh and play and learn to sit—
Bear knows where all the children go and hide
When grownups force the child too hard and wrong.
Bear loves until the heart re-opens wide
And wounds are healed which hurt the heart too long.
So grownups, hug your bears with heart's delight
And watch the ancient wrongs all turn round right!

The Sufi master Pir Vilayat Inayat Kahn praised the inner child in a talk recently. He spoke of the fact that we need new, radical ways of thinking to address the problems of the world. The creative inner child naturally has radical thinking—asking piercing questions about things grown-ups take for granted. This is what Julie did.

Overheard: Julie's Enigma

Julie and Steve were walking home from Sunday school. They were nine years old and best friends. Julie was troubled.

"I don't get why everyone likes that Bible verse that says God loved the world so much he sent Jesus to die for our sins. I hate it!" she announced emphatically, kicking a pebble with her new shoe.

"Why do you hate it?" Steve asked, only half interested. Who wanted to talk about the Bible if you didn't have to?

"Well, it talks about God's loving us and then making his son die. Seems to me, if somebody had to die, he'd do it, not make his son do it. I wouldn't like a father like that!"

Steve didn't think like Julie did. He just let things roll off his back.

"Steve, are you listening? This is important! I bet people made all that up, about God having to have somebody die to forgive us. Do you think God really needs blood—like Dracula or something?"

Steve tried to join her thoughts a bit. "Remember last fall when the teacher told us about the altars and killing and burning sheep and cows and birds so God would be pleased?"

"Ick! It makes my stomach sick," Julie shuddered. "I bet they just made it up for some reason. I bet God wonders where people get all those ideas."

There was a pause as they ambled along the shady sidewalk toward their homes. Julie stopped abruptly, her eyes intense. "Why do people like violence and killing and blood so much, Steve?" Steve was jarred. "Do you think they made that up about God because they liked to do it and decided God did, too?"

176

This was too much for Steve. "Julie, I can't understand you sometimes. Come on, I'll race you to the corner!"

Although some would say Julie's theology needs straightening out, this is the kind of fresh questioning we need for the problems that confront us—the daring, dauntless questioning of what we have believed so far. Belief is based on some kind of authority; faith is based on experience. Joseph Campbell spoke in favor of the *experience* of life:

> People say that what we're all seeking is a meaning for life. I don't think that's what we're really seeking. I think that what we're seeking is an experience of being alive, so that our life experiences on the purely physical plane will have resonances within our own innermost being and reality, so that we actually feel the rapture of being alive.

Experiencing our beautiful child—our soul—is a key to living life in harmony with our higher Self, giving the gifts we yearn to give and feeling the rapture of being alive.

CHAPTER TWELVE

Endings and Beginnings

I AM ME. . . . I own everything about me—my body, including everything it does: my mind, including all its thoughts and ideas; my eyes including the images of all they behold; my feelings, whatever they may be—anger, joy, frustration, love, disappointment, excitement; my mouth, and all the words that come out of it, polite, sweet or rough, correct or incorrect; my voice, loud or soft; and all my actions, whether they be to others or to myself. . . . I own me, and therefore I can engineer me.

—VIRGINIA SATIR

THE PATH THROUGH THE GOLDEN DOOR in the middle years requires that we gain the gifts of the connection to the true Self. Vitality, a zest for life, and a full, open heart are indicators that this connection is being built. The vitality that comes to us as we move into generativity changes our images of ourselves—we find that our self-esteem flourishes as never before.

Taking responsibility for our lives and everything we do brings a sense of empowerment. As we engage in the engineering process of shaping ourselves, the inevitable task of letting go of what no longer serves well must take place. This letting go can be likened to a death—death to old and worn out strategies.

Psychologist and family systems specialist Virginia Satir described this process of letting go and experiencing a death as entering into a time of chaos. Chaos is critical, she stated. In chaos, you can no longer go back to what was because there has been a death to the former order, nor do you know where you are going because the new life possibilities are still hidden. It is the dark time, the time of the void.

"One must have chaos in one to give birth to a dancing star," said Nietzsche. In chaos, everything is open and pregnant with opportunities. This is the part of the change process that calls for trust, care, honesty, and patience. Sometimes Satir would advise a struggling client to simply relax and breathe. A simple exercise like this can help someone in chaos. If chaos hasn't happened, said Satir, then nothing has happened.

Nature has many good illustrations of death as precursor to the new. In the life of the monarch butterfly, for example, the outer casing, which is its exo-skeleton, must be shed several times while the little creature still remains in the caterpillar stage. The monarch grows from a tiny caterpillar through several stages to a medium-large caterpillar, each time with different markings. But nature makes necessary, often hidden, preparations for each new step. Under its old covering the caterpillar develops a new and roomier container. When the time is right, the old, tight covering splits and drops away; the new expands and soon firms up. It is a much better situation—until the next time.

In the last major transformation, the monarch engages in the most awesome and vulnerable change of all. Hidden inside the chrysalis it transforms from a milkweed patch worm to a delicately strong creature that flies thousands of miles in its lifetime. No wonder the butterfly has always been a symbol of new life to all peoples of the earth.

How Our Small Breakdowns Liberate Us

Clearly the caterpillar is going through an ending—a breakdown—when its outer skeleton covering splits and the new unknown one is wet and vulnerable. Breakdown is necessary.

Larger breakdowns are another story and demand major interventions, but small ones occur regularly for us all. I offer you the following journal entries with the hope that they can help you value your times of ending. You can negotiate the process more easily when you know that there is meaning and purpose in what is happening to you.

JOURNAL ENTRIES

I am in a mini-breakdown. How do I know? Because I cry at the drop of a hat. Because life is harder than usual and the happiness I so enjoy is missing. All my compulsions are clamoring and I find myself wandering into the kitchen, opening the refrigerator door, eating greedily of its contents. My patience with people is collapsing and anger bubbles up irrationally. The harsh inner judging voices are clamoring: "You shouldn't . . . You always . . . Why don't you ever . . . "

IT'S PART OF BEING HUMAN: I am well aware of the small depressions, mini-collapses, and breakdowns which are part of being human. Earlier in life, I didn't understand what was happening in these times and I tried to pretend I was all right and life was the same as usual.

DENIAL: What I am experiencing now is subtle and has stages. I have just come through denial. When I am in denial, I am trying to keep things even, under control. I am barely aware that this is what I am doing, but it is. In order to compensate for feeling uneasy and

181

edgy, I drop my disciplines one by one. Foods that are harmful for me begin to appeal with phony promises of relief.

I seek out other short-term pleasures. Perhaps I stay in bed instead of getting up for a morning walk. I find my meditation practice bores me. These are signs that I am denying myself my real feelings and thoughts—and it follows that I deny I am in denial.

COMPELLED TO LOOK: Finally guilt and other unpleasant emotions begin to get my sluggish attention. I feel compelled to look at what I am doing. This can take days, weeks, depending on many things. I begin to look for reasons behind my self-sabotaging behaviors. At first I try to explain them away: it's been so rainy, I've been working too hard, if my husband would just. . . .

Something insists on being recognized. I begin to be aware of dreams—maybe I dream I've lost my car keys, or bandits are chasing me, or I can't find my purse, or I'm lost, or I dream of deformed and dead children. This is painful and I want to run away, hide.

I GIVE UP: Today I have moved to "I give up." At last I become open to my process. I don't understand the process but I know I am weary of fighting it (whatever "it" is). I experience how tired I am. The world looks gloomy. I feel teary and go about my life with great effort.

Questions and doubts lurk about. My belief system develops cracks and I am afraid. Once I spoke with great assurance on this and that; now, I don't know—I hate not knowing.

THE UNTHINKABLE EMERGES: All the unthinkable thoughts usually kept at bay clamor for attention. I feel my mean thoughts, critical thoughts. "Unacceptable" feelings rise up and insist I hear them out.

Tip-toeing in from the corners of consciousness at last comes a true friend, acceptance. I begin to say yes to what is happening—I surrender. My new honesty brings more balance to my life.

WORDS OF REASSURANCE: My teacher's words encourage me and I take notes: "It is healthy for you to be feeling your fears right now. You have to allow yourself to fear what you fear, feel what you feel; you can't do anything more than that."

MAKING WAY FOR SOMETHING NEW: "In breakdown, you are making way for something new to come in. When you are too full of your old and obsolete life, nothing new can enter in. A layer of nonsense needs to fall away from you. It will be an increasing blessing for you when you can no longer tolerate what is not true for you.

"Deep spiritual changes happen in their own time, like drips on a rock which wear it away. It takes time and thousands of drips. We do our little part, but so do a lot of others. We need to be honest, experience how it is."

WE NEED OUR MISTAKES: "Your errors are valuable. You need your mistakes to highlight the truth. You have to experience how error feels to begin to be free from it."

THE GREAT REWARD: "Finally, when it all falls apart and you let go, you receive the great reward. Behind what we often label as 'out of control' time lies power time—new possibilities are born.

"When you catch yourself thinking: 'Oh, I'm cracking up!' feel your process, watch yourself, develop an accepting stance of absolutely everything. Bypass the intellectual, don't try to understand! Stay in your body, feel and watch. You are a caterpillar going into a dormant period. You can feel you're suffocating, but know you are going to be a butterfly."

Letting go is a hard but necessary part of the generative process. We tend to cling to much that no longer serves us well, and breakdown can provide an essential time for surrender. There are promises inherent in our times of crisis and breakdown, and we can count on knowing that on the far side of breakdown and surrender is an inflowing of gifts. We can expect to experience a time of peaceful happiness with a pervading sense of accomplishment. Things from which we have longed to be released will be increasingly released, and that which we long to give we'll be more equipped to give. We feel empowered as love emerges healthier, richer, and clearer.

We learn to be less critical of ourselves and others when the times of mix-up and mistakes come along. We may even become wise enough to welcome these difficult times because we can trust that they are, in truth, opportunities for transformation.

The Spiral Dance:
The End Is the Beginning

Middle adulthood is full of beginnings and endings. Our task is to recognize the endings, grieve for them, and then let them go. Poet Emily Dickenson described succinctly the dance of letting go to become alive in a new way.

A death blow is a life blow to some
Who, til they died, did not alive become;

Who, had they lived, had died, but when
They died, vitality begun.

We need to prepare for the new beginning the way we would prepare for a new sport or activity. We must see if we have the ability; count the cost in time, energy, and money; equip ourselves appropriately; learn the rules, and find a good coach. When we participate in a sporting event, we lay aside extra or inappropriate clothing and baggage that would impede us.

One woman known as Peace Pilgrim in her later life remembered a time of seeking for the meaning of her life. One night she walked for hours through the woods struggling with questions—enduring the dark night of the soul that seemed like a death. As dawn came, she felt a major transition in herself; she was flooded with a complete willingness to give her life over to service. For her, it was a point of no return.

Her willingness, however, was only the beginning. Fifteen years of preparation and inner seeking followed. During those years she began to understand her two natures, her two viewpoints. One self wanted the conventional way —comfort and convenience. The other, her higher Self, wanted to break through into inner peace, freedom, and service to others.

In the midst of this struggle to let go of her lower nature, she had a mountaintop experience and felt a oneness with all creation. She knew she had been given a glimpse of her true home. Then she finally entered the third phase of her life—living constantly with inner peace.

Peace Pilgrim spent years walking all over this country, covering 25,000 miles, wearing her shirt with the words Peace Pilgrim on it. She talked to people everywhere. Her peace message was not new. It was simple ancient wisdom: overcome evil with good, falsehood with truth, and hatred with love. Peace within each of us, she taught, will bring peace in the world.

True Self Guides in Difficult Times

Peace Pilgrim had fifteen years of struggle with her two natures before attaining inner peace and the ability to serve others out of the vast resources of her true Self. The scriptures of the world's religions acknowledge this struggle. The Hindu Scriptures, the Bhagavad-Gita, from the first century B.C., give an excellent example:

Oh, let the self exalt itself,
Not sink itself below:
Self is the only friend of self,
And self Self's only foe.
For self, when it subdues itself,
Befriends itself, And so
When it eludes self-conquest, is
Its own and only foe.

So calm, so self-subdued, the Self
Has an unshaken base
Through pain and pleasure, cold and heat,
Through honor and disgrace.

The second half of life brings with it experiences that try and test us. These times are important for developing our strengths, and they hold the promises of new beginnings. My life has given me such opportunities—I'll share one with you.

THE VISITOR

It was a day of which nightmares are made. My husband, David, had just called from the Mayo Clinic in Rochester, his voice on the phone hard, abrasive: "I'm coming home, there is nothing they can do for me here." David had been noticing uncomfortable symptoms for some time, but life was full and busy and he had managed to explain them away—until now.

I called our internist. He painted a picture that was bleak. A rare, inoperable, cancerous tumor unresponsive to known medical procedures had been growing and would probably continue to grow around the base of David's spine, gradually squeezing the sensitive nerves serving his legs and other lower body organs. The cruelty of these words hit me in the stomach. Images of wheelchairs, incontinence, and chronic pain sprang unbidden to my fertile mind. Numbly, I got my car keys and purse. I was going to the grocery store because two close friends were coming for dinner.

I went to the front door of our beachside home and pushed open the screen. A flash of reddish-brown fur disappeared around the corner of the house. What was that, I wondered to myself. Slowly, I made my way toward the corner, and there, crouching tentatively in a sheltered place, was a dog, alert brown eyes observing my every move.

I knelt to be nearer the dog's height and held out my hand. Immediately the visitor moved toward me—slowly, with tail down. I allowed the encounter to continue at its own pace. Although my furry, female visitor was clearly afraid, she was also advancing, signaling that she was available for connection.

The enchanting meeting ended and I stood up to continue to the store, my movements deliberate and slow. Returning an hour later with salmon, fresh corn, salad makings, and a bottle of wine, I was surprised to see my visitor waiting quietly in front of the door. It seemed natural to invite the dog in. Seating myself on the floor, I opened to the touching communion my new friend offered. The dog's brown eyes were warm and watchful, her fine, slim nose sensitive. She had a quiet, centered way about her, and she waited to be invited before imposing her presence on me in any way.

Soon she began to explore the small kitchen area, the living room, and my study just off the living area. I watched her. This was an unusual creature. It was obvious she had been loved—her coat was rich and shiny. She had a collie face and markings, but another breed showed as well. I wonder what her name is, I thought to myself. I would name her Shanti, meaning peace. She calms me with her presence.

I unpacked the groceries, forgetting the dog as my mind returned to my pain. Poor David. What a terrible time this must be for him. We had so many plans for our older years. The children were almost grown up and we were tasting our freedom. Walking was one of our favorite hobbies, and we had enjoyed walking all over the world from the coastline of Wales to the Inca Trail high in the Andes. What could be the meaning in it all? It seemed so unfair.

Setting my swirling thoughts aside for a moment, I wondered where my guest was. I spotted her in my study. It almost seemed as if she belonged there. I was drawn to lay down on the couch and gratefully dozed off. I had endured several sleepless nights waiting for David's test results.

When I went back to the kitchen I wondered if the dog was hungry. I found something I thought she might like and put it on the floor. My guest had followed me but seemed uninterested in the food. I got a bowl of water—the dog lapped it up. Then she sniffed the food again and daintily helped herself, licking the bowl clean. I began the dinner preparations and the dog, now called Shanti in my mind, quietly lay down.

Soon welcome footsteps announced the arrival of my friends, Titia and Marianne. They entered and wordlessly put their arms around me. Their love and tears brought comfort.

When they noticed the quiet presence lying in the living room as if she belonged, they sensed something special about her—but they also wondered what I was going to do with her. I decided to call the police to see if there was a missing dog report, but I was so confused I had difficulty finding the number. When the police asked me my phone number and address, my mind went blank and Marianne had to help me. My knowledgeable therapist friend warned me to be very gentle with myself during this stressful time.

After dinner, the sunset called to us. We walked the beach in silence as the ruler of the long June day departed in gentle tones and soft breezes while the ruler of the night rose in numinous, lunar beauty. Soothed and refreshed, we turned homeward. Lighthearted humor crept back into our conversation.

Nearing the door, we noticed that Shanti was missing. She had been invited on the walk with us and accompanied us only a few paces before stopping, clearly communicating that she did not wish to go further.

Then we noticed that the screen in the front door had been forced in and Shanti had jumped through. She was waiting for us in the living room. Oh my, did she rip the screen, I wondered.

As the three of us discussed the breaking and entering, Shanti came and stood in our midst, rubbing my legs. "She wants to know if she's forgiven," Titia sensed. I knelt beside the dog and reassured her.

David was receiving the same support from the husbands of Marianne and Titia who had chosen to meet his plane and take him out to dinner. The six of us were close friends. All of us were hikers, sharing the trails, the camping, the camaraderie and the difficulties of such times. What a gift for David and me to be able to share our deepest fears and hopes with our friends now.

The men were bringing David home about midnight. The sleepy women left around ten. I couldn't sleep, but Shanti kept vigil with me. We took short walks under the stars.

When David came home, Shanti never barked—she just accepted him. I thought it best if she slept outside by the front door in a protected place. I arranged a soft blanket and a bowl of water and went to bed.

About two o'clock I heard a series of short barks, the first time I had heard Shanti's voice. I hoped this would not disturb the neighbors. The rest of the night was quiet.

Rising early, I found that Shanti had disappeared. It came to me strongly that I had been graced with a messenger, a friend to keep vigil with me in the lonely hours of that difficult day. My heart took comfort in this sign of compassion in the universe around me.

This happened about a year ago. The tumor signaled an ending of taking health and life for granted. It became our teacher. David and I are learning an essential lesson of life —to live in the *now,* which is rich, active, and full.

When we let go of how we think things "should be," accepting what is—including endings—we open ourselves to new beginnings, new transformations, to the mystery of our true Self. The gifts this brings us are more than adequate for any challenge we may face.

CHAPTER THIRTEEN

Facing Death, and
Our Aging Parents

Death, thy servant, is at my door. He has crossed the unknown
sea and brought thy call to my home. The night is dark and
my heart is fearful—yet I will take up the lamp, open my gates
and bow to him my welcome. It is thy messenger who stands
at my door.

—RABINDRANATH TAGORE

O NE TASK THAT COMES to many of us around midlife is
the challenge of caring for aging parents. As our
parents become increasingly frail, we find the roles
between us reversing. We become the parents of our parents. This happens at a time when our own aging is becoming increasingly obvious. We are called upon to face not
only our parents' physical losses and eventual death, but
also our fears around our own mortality.

Most of us have known adult children, usually women, who
have put their own goals, hopes, and activities on hold to care
for aging parents. A U.S. House of Representatives report
stated that the average American woman spends eighteen

years helping aging parents. Increasingly today, men are participating in the care-giving role as well.

The challenge of caring for our aging parents needs to be thought through carefully in light of other aspects and demands in our lives. We must be ready to help them without totally giving up our own lives in a co-dependent way. If we have engaged in the work of healing our inner child, as chapter eleven suggested, we are better equipped to sense what is really best, loving, and kind for all concerned, given the circumstances.

As parents come to the time of life when they need our help, we can expect to go through a transition ourselves. The relationship between adult children and their frail, elderly parents can be stressful, a tangle of anguish, frustration, devotion, guilt, and love.

By engaging in preparation strategies such as reading books and talking with others before the crisis of aging, ill, or dying parents confronts us, we can begin to sort out our feelings and priorities while there is space and time to think clearly. We can educate ourselves about the options that are suitable for our circumstance.

James Halpern's useful book, *Helping Your Aging Parents,* helps us become more aware of the range of responsibilities and reactions with which we may be confronted. Challenges include the need to gain an understanding of the physical and emotional changes that accompany aging and the need to educate ourselves regarding the services available in our communities. Often difficult decisions must be made about the kind of care needed and the financial demands involved.

You can begin your search by contacting your state or local office of aging. Listening to what our parents want; asking others how they are managing; expressing fears, needs, and confusions; and checking with extended family members to see how the family has historically dealt with this challenge are all helpful strategies. Seeking a support group could also be beneficial. One such group, Children of Aging Parents (CAPS), now has more than a hundred chapters across the country.

How our parents live their last years can be a profound experience for us, a time of reconciliation, perhaps, a time of increased intimacy. At the very least, it will be a learning experience from which we can benefit. We can learn from both negative and positive examples.

Death in Our Culture

The process of dying in our culture has changed dramatically in recent years. There is an incredible difference between the "typical" death of the first quarter of this century and the "typical" death in this last quarter. The process, place, and causes of dying have all changed.

Death used to be seen as a natural and logical life process event. "Letting nature run its course" was a common phrase. Today, through our medical interventions, we increasingly face ethical dilemmas. For example, are we needlessly prolonging the death process and causing unnecessary suffering?

Unfortunately, dying persons and their families have less and less control of the dying process today. One example is the case of *Cruzan vs. Harmon.* In 1983 Nancy Cruzan, age thirty-two, sank into a coma as a result of an automobile accident. Her doctors predicted she would never recover from this vegetative state. She was kept alive with food and water solutions by means of surgically implanted tubes in her stomach. This condition could potentially continue for thirty years.

After a time, Nancy's parents requested that the tubes be removed, but their request was denied by the courts up to the Supreme Court. Finally, in 1991, permission to remove the tubes was granted and Nancy was allowed to die naturally.

The Cruzan family's suffering focused national attention on the needs and rights of dying persons. We must do advance planning to ensure that our wishes will be carried out. Two documents, a Living Will and a Durable Power of Attorney for Healthcare, will assist us. A Living Will is a simple written request from you to your doctors instructing them not to put you on life-support equipment if you are hopelessly ill and want to die without further medical intervention. The Durable Power of Attorney for Healthcare is a better legal document than the Living Will. It allows you to designate your relative or close friend to make medical decisions if you become incompetent. Another document called My Medical Directive allows you to consider four medical situations you may face and to designate your wishes for medical treatment from a range of situations and options.

Many organizations and stationers supply such documents, and they can be filled out without legal advice. Make several copies of the completed documents and give to your doctors, your lawyer, your witnesses, and those who would make sure your wishes are honored.

The hospice (sometimes called palliative care) movement has helped to fill a need for people who have terminal illnesses and wish to die in their own homes. Hospice staff and volunteers are trained to be useful and comfortable around the natural process of dying. Some forward-thinking hospitals have their own homelike hospice units as a separate but integral part of their services.

The Right to Die movement also supports the dying. Two societies, the Exit Society and the Hemlock Society, have formed to combat the medical model's emphasis on life at any cost. They recognize that many people come to a time when they are ready to die.

The Hemlock Society, for example, addresses the option of rational suicide for a person in advanced terminal or serious incurable illness. With a goal of self-deliverance for the dying, they do research and publish educational materials that provide accurate information for successful self-deliverance.

Even the mainstream media have been tackling this issue. The desperation of many of our elderly who are terminally ill and who want to die with dignity—at home—served as the focus for an edition of the television news show *60 Minutes*.

Most people I have talked to concerning this important subject say that they do not fear death itself, but only a debilitating and dehumanizing illness with expensive, painful, and exhausting medical interventions. That is certainly one of my fears for myself or for someone close to me.

As a culture we are beginning to take death out of the closet and recognize that dying is an important event. Death sets a limit on our time in this life and urges us to do what we need to do in the time we are given. As Elisabeth Kubler-Ross observed, death is the final stage of growth in this life. She encourages us to begin to see death as a friendly but invisible companion, reminding us to *live* our lives and not just exist.

Dying with Dignity

What does the word "dignity" convey? Some synonyms are decorum, propriety, nobility, grace, decency. To have dignity is to have a sense of worth, poise, and respect in one's self and deportment and to function as a significant and integrated person.

How does the lack of dignity manifest in our dying practices today? Some elements may include debilitating pain either from disease or as a side effect of medical procedures. Sometimes we make too-intense attempts to live, subjecting ourselves to increased medical intervention, burdening and extending the costly time of suffering for the family as well as for us.

Sometimes material poverty or the lack of a responsible caregiver impoverishes our process, or we lose control over our lives because of stroke, coma, or life-support systems that legally cannot be removed. We can be unprepared for death—spiritually impoverished, holding onto anger, depression, and fear. Unfinished business with loved ones, holding grudges, or feeling unforgiven interferes with what could be a peaceful process. Invasive and noisy environments in hospitals or at home are debilitating to someone who is weak or sick. Isolation and abandonment by family and friends can occur.

Steven Levine in his book *Who Dies?* wrote of the need to prepare for our death. Whatever prepares us for death enhances our lives, Levine stated. The dying teach us how to live. Awareness of our mortality will facilitate important shifts in our priorities and values.

Native Americans had strategies for preparing for death. Throughout their lives, beginning at a rite of passage ceremony during adolescence, the young were taught by the wise ones to open to the unknown and receive a guiding message that would act as a touchstone for the rest of their lives. During a time of fasting and silence, young people were taught to open to the Great Spirit to receive their guiding message. It could come in a dream, from one of the old ones, or spontaneously.

The message then became a chant that was used over and over throughout life. Usually called a death chant, sometimes a healing chant, it became an integral part of each native American and was called upon whenever there was a need—in times of illness, accident, or sudden danger. As the familiar power-words were chanted they calmed and centered the chanter. Many native Americans died with clarity because they had practiced a technique that integrated life and death for them. They were prepared.

The Hindu tradition teaches that there are differences in the quality of death; a good death is courted and enhanced by having God's name on our lips. This practice will return us to our Source in the next life. There are 101 names for this Source, and people are encouraged to fill their minds with them in a prayer-chant throughout life. A good death is one in which the essence of God is with us. This practice centers and fills hearts and minds with peacefulness.

The question "Are there ways I can live now that will better prepare me for death and the possibility of another life?" can enhance our lives now. It seems reasonable, whether one believes in a next life or not, to look for answers that will afford us a sense of peace and strength to live this life with meaning and purpose.

Living the present moment fully will be the best preparation for what the future holds. For those who believe that some aspect of the human being—a soul—survives after the physical body is gone, death is viewed as a transition experience from this life to the next. It is seen as another birth into mystery, and the body can be gently and gratefully laid aside.

Much of the research on near-death experiences by Moody and Kubler-Ross lends credibility to the ancient teachings and intuitional knowings that assert there is life after death. The patients studied experienced a floating out of their physical bodies and were comforted with an overwhelming sense of peace and wholeness. Most experienced another person who greeted and helped them to the other side. Sometimes the transitional persons were loved ones who had already died; sometimes they were religious figures who were significant for the one dying. Those studied felt a warm sense of light as they were shown a panoramic playback of key events in their lives. The experience profoundly affected the rest of their lives, and death was no longer an enemy.

Two Examples to Consider

In *Necessary Losses* Judith Viorst wrote of a woman, a psychoanalyst and teacher, who was much beloved. She had kept the gifts of youth: curiosity, an interest in life and people, laughter, enjoyment of books, movies, museums, and more.

On her eightieth birthday so many people wanted to celebrate and honor her that it took five separate parties to accommodate everyone. In her presence, people felt bigger and learned to appreciate their gifts and value. "She always made you feel that you were being given something. No one ever left her empty-handed." She was a small, fragile woman, wheelchair bound and having difficulty breathing, yet "vividly alive." She died soon after her eightieth birthday, but she left a legacy. Part of the legacy was this dream she shared with a friend.

In the dream she sits at a table. She is dining with some friends and eating with pleasure, from her plate and theirs. But before she has finished her dinner, a waiter starts clearing the dishes away. She protestingly raises her hand. She wants to stop him, but then reconsiders and slowly drops her hand. She'll let him clear—she will not tell him no. Her meal isn't finished, the food still tastes good, and she'd certainly like to have more. But she knows she's full, and she's ready to let the rest go.

The promise of this fine old woman's experience encourages us to live our lives to the full, the best preparation to gently lay life aside when our time comes.

Another inspiring story of choice came from a well-known journalist and author, a man in his late eighties. He confided recently: "Sometimes I wake up in the night and feel myself hovering over my rusty, creaky old body. I look down at it lying there on the bed and I ask myself, Do I want to get back in the old carcass? Do I still have work I want to do? Or do I want to move on. So far, as you can see, I have decided to stay here."

Mother, Osteoporosis, and Alzheimer's

A friend, Marcia, watched as her once-active mother became increasingly ill and confused with Alzheimer's disease. It had not been an easy mother/daughter relationship, but Marcia had done the work necessary to let forgiveness spread its healing balm. She was now free to enjoy and accept her mother while remaining fully herself. Now a Protestant minister, Marcia shared the experience of her mother's last illness with her congregation.

201

THE COMMUNION OF THE RED SHOES

"And they were together with one accord . . ." ACTS 1:14

There is an incredible difference between knowing something with one's head and knowing it with the heart. The word "communion" has come to me recently —perhaps because there is something more to communion that I am to learn, something about living daily in the presence of God.

My mother's condition was deteriorating, and I knew she soon would be demanding more of my attention. The past two years had been a strain as osteoporosis and Alzheimer's caused my active mother to become housebound in Boston. She had taken pride in her community activities, her job as a travel agent, and her good mind. All of these were no longer available to her. She compensated by making the house her domain and closely monitoring all that came in and went out. This included Meals-on-Wheels, the mail, rubber bands, the plumber, and, of course, her two daughters. Her thoroughness was remarkable!

As I had anticipated, mother got worse. The two women who took turns caring for her were exhausted as she became more disoriented and anxious. It was time to move her out of the house. I began checking on facilities and was told to look into a home with an Alzheimer's wing.

The home turned out to be an ugly building in the middle of two busy highways. Reluctantly I spoke with the director. She began to explain the Alzheimer's wing to me. "You see, these people suffer more from isolation than from physical pain. In the Alzheimer's wing we provide a place that is safe, protected by locked doors and with a staff that doesn't expect patients to remember which is their room or what they did ten minutes ago. They interact with each other and become a community."

Two weeks later my mother moved in. We put her bedspread on a bed by one of the few windows that looked out on a hidden patio. We marked her name on her clothes and introduced her to her roommate Ophelia, whom she decided to call Ann. Every time I go to see her she introduces me to her roommate, Ann. They are becoming friends. Ann, I mean Ophelia, doesn't seem to mind her new name. If you forget someone's name when you visit, it doesn't matter, because everyone forgets names there.

As my mother is being forced by Alzheimer's to let go of the reality that she has known, I am being asked to suspend my presuppositions to enter into her world. She is teaching me about communion. As we free ourselves from the presumptions of what *ought* to be happening in our lives and in our relationships, we can become open to a new reality.

Something else is happening as I visit my mom, something that I had not expected. Often she speaks to me about her father. I get glimpses of her childhood, her hurts, and her affection for her father. She is allowing me to know her on a level I had never known her before. If I will but listen and be open to her reality, she will give me communion.

Something is shifting inside of me. My caring for my mother at this stage in her life had come out of my sense of responsibility and obligation to the one who had cared for me as I was growing up. Now I find that I truly look forward to being with her.

We laugh together. We laughed when I found that she was wearing five pairs of underpants because "people take them, you know." We laughed when she told me that one morning someone came in the room wearing her dress.

The most enjoyable time of all came after I had noticed that she was always wearing her medium high-heeled shoes and that she was walking with difficulty. I suggested she wear her slippers for a while. She said, "Oh no, not here, I'm about to go somewhere." Mother always dressed as if she were going out.

At another visit I was wearing a new pair of red loafers. She admired my shoes. Getting into the reality of the place I said, "Why don't you try them on?" Her eyes lit up, and her roommate Ann, I mean Ophelia, joined in helping her on with them. Mom admired them on her feet although they were a size too big. I suggested she try walking in them, and we walked down the hall together. She said they felt fine as they sloshed on and off the back of her heels. I admired them on her. They matched her red sweater perfectly.

I said, "I'll buy you a pair just like this in your size." She liked the idea. Then she said, "This size fits just fine."

I said, "You really like them don't you?"

She said, "Yes."

I knew what I was going to do—so I said, "Mom, why don't you keep them. They look wonderful on you." I kissed her goodbye, put on my coat, held my head up high, and walked out of there in my stocking feet. I gave her communion.

Accepting Another's Reality

Learning to accept another's reality and being able to work with that reality even when it becomes considerably different from ours is the work of intimacy—heart work. Walking in another's shoes with understanding and empathy while still connected to our own experience and reality is the work of compassion. Helping our parents as they age and die could call for this understanding compassion, and we can expect to find ourselves transformed in the process.

Generativity is dependent upon the qualities of personality that emerge out of engaging with others in an intimate way. Walking through the dying process with our parents or others can help us move on developmentally. Understanding how close relationships operate and the many pitfalls that are there for us is a big task at any time, but it becomes essential in middle adulthood.

As life moves on, the despair and disgust people often feel—associated with negative aging—come partly as a result of not learning to relate with others in a close and connected way. Although Erik Erikson delineated the time of young adulthood as the ideal time to choose between intimacy and isolation, I have found that this is a life-long challenge, a continuing process that, hopefully, is begun in early adulthood.

We can be sure that life will give us many opportunities to choose intimacy over isolation—a full, open heart over a narrow heart. Accepting the dying of another person is a teaching. The cultivation of our capacity for intimacy, so essential to generativity, helps us when we face the process of accepting another's death, or our own.

CHAPTER FOURTEEN

Remember Who You Are

Our birth is but a sleep and a forgetting;
The Soul that rises with us, our life's Star,
Hath had elsewhere its setting
And cometh from afar;
Not in entire forgetfulness,
And not in utter nakedness,
But trailing clouds of glory do we come
From God, who is our home:

—WILLIAM WORDSWORTH

OUR MIDDLE YEARS call us to become more aware of that essential, animating part of us often referred to as soul or spirit—"our life's Star." I have used the phrase "real Self" and "true Self" in this book to indicate the valuable inner core that spiritual traditions call soul or spirit.

The search for the soul connection brings no fame or glory, and many who live only in the external world would think it a foolish waste of time. Yet this is the essence so many great religions teach that lasts beyond this lifetime. It is the real seat of our power. Other forms of power—money, control of the environment, physical dominance—are types of external power. They can be stripped away, but power from within can never be lost.

Claiming this power, remembering who we really are, and experiencing a greater reality are challenges worthy of those claiming the path of living and aging successfully. When we make peace with these challenges, many other issues of our lives sort themselves out. No longer puffed up with our own cleverness, we radiate harmony and kindness. We become people with a single vision, a single purpose. Kierkegaard spoke of the "purity of heart to will one thing." Jesus taught, "Let your eye be single." The Hindus speak of this single vision as the third eye, the eye in the middle of the forehead that sees the bigger picture and is open to both the unseen and seen worlds.

To have a unifying purpose or goal does not necessarily make life easier, because our goals lead us into all sorts of unexpected places. But a unifying purpose gives us a larger perspective and the smaller pieces of life fall into place. Ultimate goals give meaning to life beyond our death, and we enjoy a purpose transcending our finite life.

We have come to accept that physical exercise is good for the overall health of the body. Exercise tones muscles, improves circulation, strengthens the heart, opens up breathing, releases toxins trapped in the body, cultivates the highly valued endorphins that bring a sense of well-being, and builds the immune system. Spiritual exercises serve much the same purpose for our inner lives; the spiritually fit have discovered the "exercise program" most harmonious with their personality, beliefs, and inclinations.

Some spiritual exercises help us to think and reason more clearly, others encourage the response of our hearts. Some ways of cultivating spiritual contact are formal and planned —worship services, organized ritual, meditation, contemplation, vocal prayer, devotions, guided reflection on one's life and behaviors, and educational events. These activities take place in homes, churches, temples, synagogues, in nature, and in sweat lodges, to name a few. They can be led by spiritual and religious teachers and leaders, therapists, shamans, artists, and others.

We also open to the divine in informal, spontaneous ways —through art, music, dance, journal writing, poetry, personal ritual (alone or with others) nature, physical exertion, dreams. We can find our soul connection through communion with others, through suffering, joy, peak experiences, deep sexual experience; and through being in the presence of birth and death.

Authentic Spiritual Experience

To describe something of what authentic spiritual experience is like, let's start with something that it is not. It is not necessarily religious. Often people confuse the religious with the spiritual. Religions can be very helpful along the spiritual path, but religious practices have their shadow side. Religions usually develop because a special teacher or prophet connected to the spiritual life suggested certain rules and beliefs to encourage others who also wanted that connection. Over time, the world's great religions have become institutionalized and there are institutional pitfalls, rigid places, and blindspots that may hinder rather than help. Some religious practices can be divisive, demeaning, manipulative, or destructive.

It is not the purpose of authentic religion to argue over which one is "right." Each great religion has served humanity, and all the great founders and teachers have been motivated by love and kindness. The spiritual is beyond religion; it is greater than religious beliefs and cannot be contained in them. Spirituality is an essential need of human nature.

209

Everything can be seen as essentially spiritual: our feelings, choices, thoughts, questions. The whole living web we call earth carries the sacred.

The concepts of spiritual and moral can be confused as well. What is considered moral behavior differs from age to age and from culture to culture. Morality consists in what one group considers right and wrong behavior.

Ethics, too, are sometimes confused with spiritual. Ethics comprises a code of behavior that represents our moral judgments. Ethics guides our behavior in everyday tasks and interactions.

Likewise, sometimes people confuse psychic ability with spiritual ability. Psychic ability is simply an additional way of perceiving, like our sense of sight or hearing. Psychic ability is a direct way of knowing and can help us better know the spiritual.

The authentic spiritual way can make use of the goodness in our moral codes, our ethical systems, and in the great religions. There is much value in the common theme of love in all religious teachings—to love well is the ultimate goal of life.

There are many paths to find love, truth, the divine. No two people will have the same soul journey. In our experience of love, our experience of peace, and our experience of the divine working in our lives we have much to share.

What Pulls Me Backwards?

We need to recognize that there are destructive forces operating in our lives. I am referring to whatever seems to pull us away from what is in our best interest. All religions deal with this destructive force. They have many names for it: illusion, ignorance, sin, attachment, poor self-image, the lower pulls of greed and desire, evil, inertia, unconscious forces, Satan, entropy, and more.

As one begins in earnest to walk the spiritual way, one's awareness of this inner warfare becomes keener. Truly useful choices and thoughts are opposed by a force that counters, "Who cares? That's just a bunch of hogwash. You can't prove any of it."

There are times when we can get so enmeshed in the counter-pulls that we are helpless on our own. At these times, we need a life-saving squad. An example of one at work is shown in Allen's story.

ALLEN NEEDED OTHERS TO HELP HIM

Allen was a talented young man who had had a difficult childhood complicated by an inheritance that came to him at age twenty-one. He began to party a lot and eventually dropped out of graduate school. Although he tried a job here and there, he became easily dissatisfied and quit all of them.

Increasingly he ignored his family until they accepted that he wanted to be left alone. Allen drank so much that the only people who would spend time with him were other drinkers.

At that point Allen's parents did step in and got him into a substance abuse center. But he did not stay. Hospitalization failed to impress Allen with what he was doing to himself. By this time his inheritance was dwindling—hospital fees ate it up. He moved to a one-room apartment. His brain became so damaged he could not carry on an intelligent conversation. At age thirty Allen came to his senses and made the humble phone call: "Dad, could you come and get me? I need help!"

His family had been learning a great deal during this troubling time. Allen's illness had been their teacher and they came to realize their part in the problem. No one person in a family has "the problem"; it is a shared situation in the family system. The unexpected phone call from Allen reawakened long dormant hopes.

The desperate family turned to people they knew who practiced prayer and meditation and asked unashamedly for them to make a one-month commitment to their son. "He is really unable to do this alone," they explained. "He needs the positive, creative prayer-energy of many to turn this situation around."

For a time, Allen's process was touch and go. But this time he did his part, and many, unknown to him, lent their support. He has now been sober for more than two years. Because Allen visited the underside of life, looked on the face of destruction and survived, he brought back gifts of clarity and vision unusual in one so young. He now has a job and is making ends meet. He can't afford a car, a VCR, or other amenities, but he has gained the strength and self-esteem that he never had before. Allen is active in Alcoholic Anonymous' twelve-step program where he meets people who have struggled as he has and who are recovering.

Allen needed others. He could not do it alone.

His story is an extreme example of a counter-energy pulling in a negative direction, but we all struggle with these opposing pulls to some extent. We know what would be good for us to do, but we don't do it. We know we should exercise—but we don't get around to it. We know we would profit from taking a workshop—but it's our day off and we'd rather sleep in. We know our eating habits are piling up problems for the future, but it tastes good right now. We know a career change would really benefit us, but don't begin the necessary explorations.

The way of discipline, courage, compassion, and service is the harder way, but incredible strengths are gained by those willing to undertake the heroic journey.

Gaining strengths calls for courage. It takes courage to change and become aware of what is really going on. The story of Will in chapter nine illustrated this. Until Will began to see that he was not living in a way that was harmonious with his true Self, he continued to use food to dull his pain. The failure to act out his true values stole his joy and his ability to contribute in ways that nourished him.

We need to form a positive self-image. Often we do not reach for our highest potential because it does not harmonize with our image of ourselves. When we were children, many of us developed a picture of ourselves as stupid, selfish, weak, ugly, unable to carry through, or lacking in this or that. Because all those big people, like parents and teachers, told us these things, we decided they were true to some extent. We formed poor self-images and we continue to cling to them.

To live well and mature successfully we must let go of the inferior notions of ourselves and reach out for our strengths. The first step in overcoming the counter-pull is honesty—to admit we are being drawn backwards, that we are failing, dissatisfied, and not in control.

Where Is the God of Love Now?

Besides the pull against our progress, we all have had difficult experiences of loss, tragedy, and suffering. We see suffering and inequities all over the world as well, as the TV news stations pull tragic stories and pictures into our living rooms. Looking at the problems and suffering in ourselves and the world, we wonder, Where is a loving God now?

"Life is both dreadful and wonderful," says Vietnamese Zen master Thich Nhat Hanh. Although life is full of suffering, there is much beauty. The sunrise is awesome, the tree tossing in the wind hums a song, the creek skips along over the rocks, the baby smiles with winsome delight at its mother. Nhat Hanh reasoned in his book, *Being Peace,* that if we are not happy or peaceful, it is impossible to share happiness and peace with others. Just being aware of suffering would be an injustice to life. We are left with so many questions—we must learn to live with our questions and befriend the paradoxes, sorting out where we are called to contribute.

Generative people have come to accept that life is both dreadful and wonderful. They learn to use their dark night of questions to let go of their own ideas of how things should be and to increase their faith in life and the love that undergirds it. They learn to accept—even welcome—ambiguity and difficulty because so many strengths can be cultivated during these times. They also know that the dark times will be balanced by times of playfulness, effortlessness, joy.

Many of us have not reached that level where we welcome difficulties. We sometimes feel lost in the darkness, plagued by doubts. We feel afraid around the mystery of what it all means and wonder if we could have avoided some of our suffering if only we had known better. To be aware that dangerous pitfalls exist and to take every precaution to stay on safe ground is basic to claiming the harvest that comes with richly aging, but sometimes we need protection from life's disasters.

Many cultures have developed protection practices. Native American teachings include the making of shields that are decorated with symbols of protective power. Many people use power chants as protection. One example is an ancient Welsh Rune that is a favorite with people in my workshops.

In this fateful hour, I call upon all Heaven with its power,
And the sun with its brightness
And the snow with its whiteness
And the fire with all the strength it hath
And the lightning with its rapid wrath
And the winds with their swiftness along their path
And the sea with its deepness
And the rocks with their steepness
And the earth with its starkness
All these I place—by Heaven's almighty help and grace
Between myself and the powers of darkness!

Choosing and carrying some simple symbol of love with you is a useful reminder that you are not alone. The New Testament speaks of putting on the armor of God to stand against fiery darts. This armor is made of awareness of peace, love, grace—so good thoughts can protect. The book of five-thousand-year-old Chinese wisdom, the *I-Ching*, counsels, "The best way to fight evil is to make energetic progress in the good." Seeking the good and being with people of love and peace is always powerful protection.

Time-honored spiritual exercises help us toward our goal of recognizing our errors, finding protection, and opening to a higher way. The great religions guide us to surrender our ideas of how it "should" be so we can begin to see how it really is. Letting go helps release us from foolish arrogance and adolescent superiority, making way for compassionate acceptance toward all.

Surrender is essential to personal and planetary healing. Ecology must now be central to spirituality—we are now integral players in the cosmic story. By healing the earth and our relation to it, we heal ourselves and protect our children's future.

After discovering the spiritual path that seems appropriate, we can undertake disciplines that are designed to help us open to life while also protecting us from the counterforce. Prayer and meditation are disciplines on our life journey toward our spiritual center.

Prayer and Meditation

Some people speak of prayer, others of meditation, when attempting to describe the process of opening to and communing with the Ultimate. By prayer we may mean that we feel drawn to a personal God. In prayer we usually begin with expressing our needs and desires; we pray for others, for our world. Eventually we may turn to a contemplative, quiet, listening prayer.

Meditation is both similar and different and can be described as a dedication to holding the mind still, quieting down so that what is deeper and godlike can emerge unimpeded. Meditation is a stopping of action in balance with remaining alert to the experience of our true Self. India's great teacher on such matters, Saytha Sai Baba, viewed the trip into self-understanding and the experience of opening to the divine as the same journey. "Self-realization is God-realization," he stated succinctly.

When we do the hard work of meditation, we realize just how jumbled our minds can be. A classic method of orienting the mind to stillness involves focusing on a simple object or repeating a phrase like "God is love" or "Who am I?" over and over. Saying a phrase, or mantra, as some call it, helps us focus the mind on the presence of God. Many like to repeat prayers while holding beads, as the Catholics, Hindus, and Buddhists do.

In meditation one needs to slow down, change to a lower gear, as we confront our racing minds. Buddhists speak of the mind like a monkey swinging from subject to subject, yanking us here or there without pattern. Meditation also can be challenging because we come face to face with ourselves. St. Ignatius in the 1500s spoke of desolation and consolation in meditation. We need to accept whichever comes to us, desolation or consolation, because it has something important to offer us.

Teachers of prayer and meditation have always encouraged attention—mindfulness—to the breath. I used to be bored with all those admonitions to concentrate on my breath and allow it to lead me. I wanted to get on with my activities! Now I feel the power of this practice. My breath is always with me, steady and present. I can live without water, food, and warmth far longer than I can live without breath. How we receive the breath, the free air, into our bodies is symbolic of the way we receive life—with fullness or shallowness.

Even practicing attentive breathing for only twenty breaths a day teaches me much about my own mind and about God's eagerness to meet me across any bridge that I build. My breath is such a bridge, in-out, in-out. Twenty times, and things begin to change, a new perspective has a chance to creep across my anxieties. I feel calmer and more in touch with my Self after just twenty mindful breaths.

In both prayer and meditation the first requirement is to be willing, even eager, to engage in the disciplines required.

One benefit in the second half of life is that we appreicate the value and power of discipline, no longer odious. We acknowledge it to be the pathway to freedom and to gain what we truly want.

The key to meditation is practice. How do we practice? One response is that in both prayer and meditation we need quiet. It is useful to make a special place in your home for your practice. Setting up a little altar can be a simple affair. When I began, I used an end table in the tiny apartment I had—just a place for a candle, a plant or flower, and a symbol or two of my spiritual journey like a shell or loved verse or picture. Some people I know have given a whole room for this purpose. They made it a beautiful and comfortable space with inspiring pictures on the walls and an altar along one end.

Different Faiths, One Way

Tibetan Buddhist monks greet strangers who come to their temples with the question, "Welcome friend, from what noble spiritual tradition do you come?" Throughout Asian countries like India and Nepal the salutation on everyone's lips is "Namastae," accompanied by a bow with hands together as in prayer. Namastae means "I salute the God within you."

Pir Vilayat, the Sufi master, said, "Seek not for the perfect belief, but let your faith grow as you test and find what works for you, as you *experience* God in your life." Faith rests on *knowing* with your deepest inner knowing—no one can take that away. Beliefs, in contrast, rely on outer authority and may not resonate with one's inner experience.

A symbol that helps me understand how the diverse paths of religion are connected is the wheel described in

Conscious Choice by Jim Kenny. It is a great wheel, with beautifully crafted spokes and an immense rim. In the center where the spokes meet is the hub, made of the brilliant blue of empty sky. It represents the common source and the deepest level of tradition—at this point unity and promise are fulfilled.

Each spoke of the wheel is uniquely shaped and symbolizes one of the world's great religious paths. The wheel's rim represents the most superficial level of involvement in one's spiritual understanding and tradition. When we are at the entry level, the outer point on our chosen religious path, it seems as though the others are far away and strange. If I am a Buddhist standing at the rim, I find Christian practices and beliefs incomprehensible. If I am a Christian at the entry level, Moslem and Hindu rituals and symbols appear strange. As seekers move along one of the spokes from the gigantic rim to the small hub they grow in understanding and wisdom—the distance that once separated them begins to diminish.

In this sacred wheel, the outer rim is needed as well as the inner. We need the diversity, color, and pageantry of the great outer rim as well as the convergence, unity, and shared symbols of the inner.

Teachings on Transcendence

One of the reasons we seek the spiritual way is to overcome knotty problems in our lives. We acknowledge a continuing yearning for union and love, for kindness as the law of life.

Indigenous peoples over the ages and around the world have developed stories and myths to illustrate and perpetuate their beliefs and teachings. These bring forward essential

219

and time-transcending truths informed by roots deep in the collective soul of humanity. Here are the origins of the world's great religions. Like voices echoing through the centuries, refined and shaped along the way, they provide insight and perspective on human relationships and what comes after death.

Spiritual traditions encourage wisdom and prayer or meditation. They help us appreciate the role of suffering in achieving wisdom and that suffering can be a powerful teacher awakening us to our deeper lives.

We experience different kinds of suffering. One type is unproductive and meaningless, rooted in hurt pride and self-pity. Another kind is essential in overcoming the false-self system each of us has constructed. This useful suffering brings a needed end to old and useless ways. When we endure we find all will be well for us again, as we gain freedom from the will to dominate things, people, and even our own lives.

The Unexplainable

Walking the terrain of the physical and the spiritual worlds invites mystical, unexplainable experiences into our lives. One such event came to David and me several years ago. It interrupted our usual pattern of thinking and turned things upside down for a time.

AN INTERRUPTION

Spring caressed the air, flirting with the diminishing winter. We had enjoyed a playful, relaxing day in the dune country bordering Lake Michigan's southeastern shore.

On a balmy, windless day, the great lake rested mirror-like from her winter labors. Fifteen- to twenty-five-foot ice mountains that formed a collar along the shoreline in response to winter's dictatorship were slowly melting under the sun's caresses. It was the time of promise between winter and spring.

As this delectable Saturday came to a close, we decided to walk the beach and experience closely the beauty of day bowing out while night crept in. The sky was responsive to the setting sun—clear, cloudless, and shimmering. As we walked, our light-hearted conversation gave way to silence and we each withdrew into private worlds, wooed to other dimensions by the magic of the moment.

About two miles down the beach we turned around, almost with one accord. The reflected colors on ice, lake, and sky were giving way to night. The ice mountains gradually took on silhouette forms, enhancing the moonscape quality of deserted beach, rock, sand, and dune.

Suddenly I was jolted from my reverie. A soundless display caught my eye—an iridescent, blue-red light streaming from the darkening heavens, falling, falling. In shock, a moment passed before I could find my voice. "Look!" I gasped, pointing. David caught a glimpse of the bright sphere as it fell closer and closer, then disappeared behind an ice mountain. We stared for some seconds before continuing our walk. "What could it have been?" "Maybe a tail-light fell off a jet?" "A meteor?" "Maybe a UFO?" "A sign or message?" Our imaginations staggered.

Reflectively walking, we approached a clearing where lake met shore. At that moment and breathlessly close,

221

the vibrant orb rose out of the water about twenty-five feet, soundlessly split into three equal parts, and arced back down. No ripple responded at the place where the light emerged from the calm and silent water. No sound or ripple occurred where it reentered or perhaps burned out.

Amazed, awestruck, I could say nothing. David reacted differently. Recovering quickly, he went to the shoreline, cupped his hands, and called out, "Whoever you are, we are willing to communicate with you. . . . " Silent, the moment hovered. We waited, but the mystery did not reveal itself further.

Night was completing her entrance; stars appeared overhead in their reassuring patterns. Two reverent people thoughtfully climbed the beach stairs to their home.

"'Tis Not Too Late to Seek a Newer World"

Lord Tennyson wrote of Ulysses as an old man addressing his companions on their long sea voyage and remembering the times he has suffered greatly, both alone, and with those who loved him. Recognizing the unity of it all, he says, "I am a part of all that I have met." He passes on his wisdom: "How dull it is to pause, to make an end, to rust unburnished, not to shine in use."

Ulysses honored his years. He was richly old, and he sensed that some noble work was yet his, a work that becomes one who has "strove with Gods." Although he recognized that time inevitably makes the aged weak and the days remaining short, a strength of will remains. "Tho' much is taken, much abides—'Tis not too late to seek a newer world."

So too for us, who, in the second half of life, are engaging in living well, in maturing generativity. By accepting our

222

aging and the fact that much has been taken, we free our-selves to wield the considerable power we have developed —the power to influence and pass the benefits of our experi-ence on to others. We are freer now to seek a new world, to speak out against social injustice, to stand for fairness and mercy. We have more leverage and know-how than when we were young, and less to lose than our younger contem-poraries when we take unpopular positions. We can take less compromised stands than they, speaking honestly both in small ways and big. We can contribute to building a better world, giving gifts that last beyond our lifetime. Loving ra-diance flows from us, and people want to be with us.

The second part of the book has described the golden door through which we must pass to enjoy the rewards of living well and maturing successfully. We may feel as though we are looking at a great or even ominous wall as we peer into the future. Yet every wall that confronts us along the way has its golden door. It may take us a while to dis-cover the door, but it always becomes visible when we are ready to see.

This is the promise I leave with you. There is a golden door for you, a door to the future that you desire at your deepest soul level—the level where you remember who you really are. That door leads you to a future that is your birth-right: a rich and rewarding second half of life.

Activities that
Invite Generativity

T HE FOLLOWING SUGGESTIONS are meant to help stimulate your thinking. As you live with the question "What behaviors and activities will help me fulfill the promise of my life?" you will want to sort out what will hinder and what will speed you on your way. You can remind yourself of the Gandhian wisdom: never give up anything unless what you want in its place means more to you than what you are giving up.

As you read, see if anything "grabs" you, that you give an "aha" response to. Let that be your guide and let the rest go. Another suggestion: Go over the lists and sort them into a four- category checklist for: (1) What I have accomplished (2) What I am moving into, (3) What could be my dream, and (4) What is not for me.

Physical

Develop a daily exercise strategy that is *fun*. Just a walk around the block each day is a beginning.

Plan vacations with physical exercise built in.

If you play a musical instrument, wield a paintbrush, or do some other arts or crafts, hone your skills. If you never have dabbled in the arts, try it.

Get regular checkups and be knowledgeable about cholesterol levels, blood pressure, heart rate, etc.

Become aware of your addictions: caffeine, alcohol, food, tranquilizers, other drugs, sports, work, sex, busy-ness, TV, certain relationships. We are all addicted in one way or another.

Move toward moderation; small improvements count!

Find a massage therapist who will increase your wellness through safe, therapeutic touch; trade back rubs with your spouse or friend.

Know today's nutrition principles; dare to break old, un-healthy cooking and eating patterns. (Small changes count here, too.)

Enjoy fruits, veggies, grains; reduce meat, salt, fat, and sugar intake.

Develop new food pleasures by noticing color, texture, smell.

Enjoy lots of water, maybe with a lemon or lime slice in it.

Be aware that your body never lies. Learn its language and listen to its signals care-fully.

Learn how your body responds to the people and activi-ties in your day. When does it tense? What part tenses—your stomach, your jaw?

Relish your breath, taking pleasure in free fresh air.

Learn the pleasure of being "embodied"; often we are cut off from our bodies by living in our heads or in unconscious emotional pain, and we abuse the miracle we live in.

Lower your thermostat in the winter, and refrain from using air conditioning so much in the summer. It's better for you, and better for the earth.

Fill out a Living Will and a Durable Power of Attorney for Healthcare.

Encourage your parents to fill these out as well.

Sort out and pass along the things from your attic, garage, basement, closets that you no longer use. This is a symbol of clearing out your life, of making room for the new. Besides it is generous!

Financial

Review your career path and goals.

Consider your options. Just considering options can be liberating.

Get a sense of what you really *want* to do, then take a little step toward it and see what happens.

Seek counseling for a second or third career.

Work up a new resumé.

Dare to consider that you can have a job that harmonizes your political, personal, and spiritual goals.

Let what you love become more clear to you—then begin to do what you love. The work-joy dichotomy will disappear.

Consider the error that work is for wealth and wealth brings happiness.

Dare to consider change; considered risk can be very useful.

Check into financial planning strategies, be financially aware, and have a realistic plan.

Be open about money with your family or close trusted friends; discuss financial topics. Help bring finances "out of the closet."

Give money away—even a little bit opens up something wonderful for you.

Discuss inheritance matters with parents and children. Maybe clarity will help avoid distressing future difficulties.

Anticipate the breakup of the the parental home and that redistribution of possessions can bring challenges. Become clear about what items are really important for you to pass on, and then negotiate ahead of time with siblings and others. It can even be fun, sharing why a particular piece is important to you and the childhood memories it evokes.

Aging parents can bring financial burdens. Plan ahead; seek advice from experts and friends. Be aware of community resources.

Be open to letting go of the house when the children grow up and move away. Smaller quarters frees up money, time, and energy so you can focus on what is really important for you now.

Invest in people, financially—with thought and caring. Sometimes a little bit turns the tide of a life.

Mental

Educate yourself on your stage of life, your life tasks.

Become realistically aware of resources and constraints in your life.

Attend workshops in your fields of interest.

Take classes at your local library, museums, YWCA, YMCA, community college, church, university, or workplace.

Think, and reflect—develop depth and farsightedness. Consider your behaviors and those of your country and see how they will shape the future—yours, mine, and those coming after us.

Develop a partnership with truth—seek to understand the roots of current difficulties and problems.

Become a "truth seer" and a "truth sayer."

Read useful, fun, informative books; join a book discussion group.

Join a singing or music group.

Read beautiful poetry and literature. Memorize a phrase or verse that speaks to you and repeat it regularly. This stimulates your mind and soothes your spirit.

Learn the skill of discernment: when to say yes, when to say no.

Seek people who challenge your beliefs, your thinking. There is value in diversity.

Monitor your mind. Become aware of what you say to yourself in your self-talk and change thought patterns toward beneficial ones.

Consciously try to be truthful in communications with others using kindness as your guide. Sometimes we have to risk another's short-term displeasure to be faithful to what we deeply believe in.

Support yourself by honoring your own responses, needs, and interests, taking time to sort them out with compassionate attention.

Stick up for yourself. Be authentic with others in appropriate ways; doormats and martyrs end up being angry. Recognize and meditate on the lies you are living and communicating now, but without judgment. Just notice how you believe they protect you.

Understand the real Self you are. See if this is the self you present to the world.

Make lists of what you *really* want to do, have, give and be.

Emotional

Do a life review. See the major stepping-stones of your life journey. Consider where you have chosen well; then notice where your blind spots have been, where you have sabotaged yourself.

Consider the choices now before you.

Make a list of all the things you like about yourself—your talents, gifts, preferences, accomplishments.

Dream some dreams about what you'd like to do and be. Don't let financial, educational, or time considerations enter in at this stage. Just let yourself dream.

Write down a dream and see if it begins to have vitality and life beyond what you expected. Watch for breakthroughs and validations and move on them.

Dare to have your feelings, all of them—without judgment—knowing you do not have to act them out negatively.

Find creative ways of recognizing, using, and releasing feelings. Write them down with fervor and honesty. Burn them later if necessary. Share with a counselor or wise friend. If you sing or play an instrument, use this resource as therapy. Dare to be real about the darker side of your life.

Ask your family or friends how they see you. This requires courage, but they can be a mirror to reflect you to yourself.

Look at your generational family system and get a sense of trends, pitfalls, and resources in your lineage.

Go to twelve-step or other support groups if necessary. They can be that—a support! Shop around to find the right group of people for you.

Take an inventory of your relationships and be aware of your patterns with others. Take considered steps toward reconciliation as indicated (for your own sake and theirs).

Forgive yourself your mistakes—a very big task.

Forgive others their mistakes—also a big task.

Seek people who share your interests and invite them into your life.

Open yourself to making new friends.

Learn to embrace your inner child.

Take your inner child to the park or the ball game. Buy your child an ice cream cone.

Get a dog or a cat.

Write your inner child a letter, telling how much she or he is loved now. Notice how easily the tears come when your little child part has your compassionate attention. Spontaneous joy is hiding behind the tears.

Buy a teddy bear!

Explore the wonders of counseling and therapy. Courage is required to really look at one's self. A personal guide in this process is beyond price.

Enjoy the many excellent self-help books available; discuss the useful parts with a friend or spouse.

Recognize and embrace all that is beautiful in life.

Spiritual

Take the spiritual side of life seriously.

Make time to explore spiritual and religious ways.

Humbly seek help and protection from God and others in your explorations.

Seek the companionship of others who are on the spiritual way. Choose a worship group that supports your spiritual vision, needs, and goals.

Study the saints and sages of your religious tradition. Then, study those of other great traditions.

Inventory your life and see who might be a friend/teacher/guide as you explore your spiritual Self. Be aware; there are fakes, so use judgment.

Read from the great spiritual works.

Plan your "spiritual exercise" program and practice.

Practice forgiveness. It changes everything, and its rewards are permanent.

Be less concerned about the "right" belief system and cultivate an awareness of your *experience* of the spiritual.

Practice spiritual disciplines that might aid you:

- Take time for quiet reflection
- Let nature teach and nourish you
- Incorporate meditation and prayer into your life
- Maintain a personal journal
- Pay attention to dreams, writing them down and finding someone to share them with
- Practice an open attitude so something new can be born.

Make an altar or worship center in your home: a small table with a candle to signify the light, a flower or plant to bring beauty, a verse or picture to inspire you, a statue of a religious figure or some symbol to nourish you.

Reach Out

Let yourself become aware of what is happening in the environment (a painful and difficult task). Feel it.

Let yourself become aware of what is happening to earth's children, another painful recognition.

Study what the military is up to. Are their expenditures justified?

Be a watchdog on government. You can make a difference! Even one letter has impact.

For yours and others' well-being, look for opportunities to serve. Be discriminating and seek what is really right for you.

Check the lives of the young people in your family system or neighborhood. Perhaps a niece or nephew or other young person has needs you would enjoy fulfilling.

232

Take stands for peace, justice, and nonviolence; consider where you have leverage and use it to make a difference.

Check service and arts organizations in your community-donate time and money when it seems vital for you.

Practice conserving. Live more simply; recycle, take bags with you to the grocery (use string bags as the Europeans do).

Simple conservation measures can start a needed trend. For example, use only white paper products: legal pads, paper towels, toilet paper, etc., the dyes are a problem; no styrofoam; enjoy cloth napkins; walk more; ride your bicycle.

Share your ecological concerns and ideas with others.

Support the acceptance of a smaller, interdependent world.

Look at the organizations that focus on service around the world. These can offer unusual ways to travel and serve as well.

Seek out people from diverse cultures and learn from them. Compassionate outreach serves both you and another.

Follow your vitality. Do only those activities that are energy efficient for you, leaving you with a healthy tiredness, not depleted. Enjoy what you do!

Notes

Introduction

Jung wrote often of the Self, for instance in *Modern Man in Search of a Soul,* New York: Harcourt, Brace, 1933.

Kahlil Gibran's maxims were collected and edited by Joseph Sheban in *The Wisdom of Gibran,* New York: Philosophical Library, 1966, preface.

CHAPTER ONE
Successful, Unsuccessful Aging

Victor Frankl, *Man's Search for Meaning,* New York: Washington Square, 1963, preface.

Carl Jung on the absence of preparation is in *Modern Man in Search of a Soul.*

When is midlife? Researchers included R. Gould, E. Jacques, D. Levinson, V. McCoy, S. Merriam, and B. Neugarten.

"The Truth Shop," in Anthony de Mello's *The Song of the Bird,* (New York: Image Books, 1984) is one of the illustrative parables he collected from diverse cultures and religions.

Charles Dickens's classic *A Christmas Carol* was published in December 1843. It was an instant success and has remained so, year after year. Clearly it touches people of all ages in a continuing and deep way (Chalfont, PA: Byers Choice, 1989).

Cultural anthropologist and author Angeles Arrien teaches at the Institute of Transpersonal Psychology, Menlo Park, California.

CHAPTER TWO
Growing Older Richly—through All Life's Stages

Henry David Thoreau, *Walden,* New York: Signet Classics, The New American Library, 1960.

"Eight Ages of Man" in Erik Erikson's *Childhood and Society* and *The Life Cycle Completed,* New York: Norton, 1950 and 1982, chapters 7 and 3, respectively.

Judith Viorst, "What am I doing with a mid-life crisis?" *Necessary Losses,* New York: Fawcett, 1986, 298.

Facing our darker aspects and the shadow is emphasized by many authors; Murray Stein in *MidLife* (Dallas: Spring Publications, Inc., 1983) and Roger Gould in *Transformations* (New York: Simon & Schuster, 1972) are two.

Jung, *Modern Man in Search of a Soul.*

The qualities of successful and unsuccessful aging come from research for my dissertation, *Generativity In Middle Adulthood* (1985), and from a national survey of 567 people ages 40–75 who voluntarily responded to questionnaires designed by myself in cooperation with Market Facts, Inc., of Chicago. This study done in 1986.

CHAPTER THREE
Choices, Changes, More Choices

The Serenity Prayer is used in all the twelve-step programs.

"The Road Not Taken" from *The Poetry of Robert Frost,* edited by Edward Lathem, New York: Holt, Rinehart, 1970.

Everyday tasks are compiled from my research and that of C. Buhler, R. Gould, D. Levinson, B. Neugarten, G. Vaillant, and others.

Ortega Y Gasset, from *Some Lessons in Metaphysics,* New York: Norton, 1969.

Moses, Deut. 30:19.

CHAPTER FOUR
Lives to Learn From

William Wordsworth, "My Heart Leaps Up," in *Harvard Classics,* 61 Ed. Charles Elliot, New York: P.F. Collier & Son, 1910, volume 41.

The study: *Generativity In Middle Adulthood* (1985).

John Bradshaw's books, *Healing the Shame that Binds You,* and *Coming Home,* can provide more insight on the extent of our childhood wounds and ways to encourage the healing process. He also has useful audio and videotapes on the family.

CHAPTER FIVE
Entry into Midlife

Carl Jung, "Stages of Life," in *Modern Man in Search of a Soul,* 108.

CHAPTER SIX
Risks and Consequences

Rollo May, *The Courage To Create,* New York: Norton, 1972, 4.

CHAPTER SEVEN
A Delightful Quality of Personality

Abraham Maslow, *Further Reaches of Human Nature,* New York: Viking, 1971, 43.

For more information on finding a way to harmonize your personal, political, and spiritual ideals with your income-producing endeavors see Naomi Stephan's work *Finding Your Life Mission,* Walpole, N.H.: Stillpoint Publishing, 1989, and Marsha Sinetar's book *Do What You Love The Money Will Follow,* New York: Dell Publishing, 1987.

The quote by Rumi I heard at a conference and memorized it instantly.

CHAPTER EIGHT
"I Make a Difference"

The Hundredth Monkey Phenomenon is in *The Hundredth Monkey,* by Ken Keyes, Jr. (Coos Bay, OR: Vision Books, 1987).

The story of Teddy and Ms. Thompson was transcribed from "An Hour of Good News," televised on WTTW January 12, 1986, by Dr. Anthony Campolo, Jr., sociologist and chair of his department at Eastern College in Pennsylvania. I took the story from the transcript.

The information from Dan Goleman was part of a talk given at a conference sponsored by the East-West Foundation in 1989. Using examples from world problems, he illustrated how we get caught in self-deceptions and that living in denial too long is endangering life on this planet. His book *Vital Lies, Simple Truths* (New York: Simon & Schuster, 1985) explores this concept further.

Sigmund Jahn (German Democratic Republic) in *Noetic Sciences Review,* 7 (Summer 1988), 18. It is a quote from *The Home Planet,* a book conceived and edited by Kevin Kelley and co-published by both U.S. (Addison-Wesley, 1988) and USSR firms.

The information on community movements around the earth is from Allen Durning's "Mobilizing at the Grassroots," in *State of the World, 1989,* New York: Norton, 1989, chapter 9.

For information on the "new physics," I drew from Gary Zukov's book *The Dancing Wu Li Masters* (New York: William Morrow, 1979) and Fritjof Capra's *Tao of Physics* (Berkeley: Shambhala, 1975).

The quote by Astronaut Edgar Mitchell was also in the Noetic Sciences Review.

Margery Williams, *The Velveteen Rabbit.* This edition is illustrated by Michael Hague. The illustrations are very special (New York: Holt, Rinehart, 1983, 4, 5).

CHAPTER NINE
Life: A Generous Giver

Rainer Maria Rilke, *Letters to a Young Poet* translated by H. Norton, New York: Norton, 1954, 29, 30.

G. Spencer Brown, *Laws of Form,* London: George Allan & Unwin, 1969, 110.

The Sufi Byazid wisdom was in Anthony De Mello's *The Song of the Bird,* 153.

Whitehead and Whitehead, *Christian Life Patterns,* New York: Image Books, 1979.

There are not many books on friendship. I can recommend, however, an excellent one: Lillian Rubin's book *Just Friends,* New York: Harper & Row, 1985.

"Freely Offered Gifts" came to me on a Christmas card years ago. I saved it.

The story on "Good luck, bad luck, who knows?" is an ancient tale from China. I have seen it in several different versions.

CHAPTER TEN
Family Dynamics and Our True Self

The old hymn is one my father and grandfather liked. As a child I memorized it.

The Dalai Lama's thoughts are taken from a 1989 conference I attended sponsored by the East-West Foundation. The Dalai Lama spoke with a panel of scientists and psychologists for three days.

Riane Eisler, *The Chalice and the Blade,* San Francisco: Harper & Row, 1987.

Harriet Lerner, *The Dance of Anger,* particularly Chapter 2 (New York: Harper & Row, 1985).

CHAPTER ELEVEN
The Child of Yesterday, the Adult of Today

Lao Tsu, *Tao Te Ching* from about the sixth century B.C.

"I Am Cherry Alive," by Delmore Schwartz, was illustrated and made into the children's book *"I am Cherry Alive," the Little Girl Sang* by Barbara Cooney. It is so beautiful and the artwork so compelling I have used it to meditate on (New York: Harper & Row, 1979).

Charles Whitfield wrote *Healing the Child Within,* a useful book on discovering the inner child for adults from dysfunctional families (that describes a lot of us!). (Deerfield Beach, FL: Health Communications, Inc., 1987).

The quote from Socrates I saw on a poster at an art fair.

All Alice Miller books are shocking as they raise our awareness of the hidden cruelty in child-rearing practices. *For Your Own*

Good and *Thou Shalt Not Be Aware* are compelling (New York: Farrar, Straus, 1983, 1981).

Lynn Andrews' books teach us some of the wisdom of the native American medicine healers. I especially liked *Flight of the Seventh Moon* (San Francisco: Harper & Row, 1984). It contains teachings about the shields and their protective and spiritual powers.

Joseph Campbell & Bill Moyers, *The Power of Myth,* New York: Doubleday, 1988.

CHAPTER TWELVE
Endings and Beginnings

Virginia Satir, *Peoplemaking,* Palo Alto, CA: Science and Behavior, 1972, 27–29.

Nietzsche's quote is from a T-shirt I saw at an art fair. I copied it on the spot.

Emily Dickinson's poem is in the anthology *The Choice Is Always Ours,* Wheaton, IL: Re-Quest Books, 1977, 44. I recommend this book as a treasure chest of wisdom from around the world.

The Peace Pilgrim story is from *Yoga Journal* "Peace Pilgrim's Progress," (January–February 1990), 104.

The quote from the Bhagavad-Gita, the "New Testament" of the Hindu Scriptures, is in *The Choice Is Always Ours* edited by Dorothy Phillips, 41.

CHAPTER THIRTEEN
Facing Death, and Our Aging Parents

Rabindranath Tagore, from Gitanjali, LXXXVI. From Elisabeth Kubler-Ross, *On Death and Dying,* New York: MacMillan, 1969, 181.

Helping Your Aging Parents by James Halpern is a practical guide for adults with aging parents. It is fairly comprehensive and can help you offer support without giving up your life (New York: Fawcett Crest, 1987).

Steven Levine's book *Who Dies?* comes out of his work with the dying beginning with Kubler-Ross. He now works with Ram Dass as director of the Hanuman Foundation Dying Project. I am indebted to him for this compassionate and skillful book on the mystery of dying (New York: Doubleday, 1982).

Kubler-Ross has also written *Death the Final Stage of Growth.* I drew from her work and from the work of Raymond Moody, Jr. M.D., who wrote *Life after Life* (New York: Bantam, 1975).

Necessary Losses, 330. I recommend her whole book.

Marcia Heeter preached "The Communion of the Red Shoes" at Winnetka Presbyterian Church on November 22, 1987.

CHAPTER FOURTEEN
Remember Who You Are

Wordsworth, "Ode on Intimations of Immortality from Recollections of Early Childhood," in *Harvard Classics,* 609. Almost two hundred years old, the entire poem is blessed with wisdom and "thoughts that do often lie too deep for tears."

For some thoughts in the Authentic Spiritual Experience section, I am indebted to Rachel Remen. See *Noetic Sciences Review* (Autumn 1988).

Being Peace (Berkeley, CA: Parallax, 1987) is excerpted from talks given on a tour. Nhat Hanh is committed to helping refugees worldwide. He was nominated for the Nobel Peace Prize by Dr. Martin Luther King, Jr. (Berkeley, CA: Parallax, 1987).

The Welsh Rune was taken from Madeleine L'Engle's children's series "The Time Quartet." She wove the story in *A Swiftly Tilting Planet* around the ancient saying (New York: Farrar, Straus, & Giroux, 1979).

Jim Kenny, "The Sacred Wheel: Vow and Blessing," *Conscious Choice* (Fall 1989), 30–31.

Alfred Lord Tennyson, "Ulysses," in *Harvard Classics,* 1007–1009. This poem is filled with wisdom!

About the Author

PAULA HARDIN obtained her doctorate in education from Northern Illinois University with a research emphasis on adult development, particularly the choices of midlife that shape the second half of life. For her post-doctoral master's in pastoral studies from Loyola University, she focused on stages of spiritual development as found in religious literature.

The director of her own business, Midlife Consulting Services, Paula also teaches, lectures, and writes. She and her husband, David (who freely admit to not having it all together), find life more rewarding now at ages 58 and 64 than ever before. They love to hike, and this love has taken them to unusual places around the world. They have a blended and extended family that provides many opportunities for growth.

Permissions

Anthony de Mello, "The Truth Shop" and "Change the World by Changing Me" in *The Song of the Bird*. New York: Image Books, 1984. Reprinted by permission.

Judith Viorst, "What am I Doing with a Midlife Crisis?" and the old woman's dream in *Necessary Losses*. New York: Fawcett, 1986. Reprinted by permission.

Harriet Lerner, from *The Dance of Anger*. New York: Harper & Row, 1985. Reprinted by permission.

Delmore Schwartz, "'I Am Cherry Alive' the Little Girl Sang." New York: Harper & Row, 1979. Reprinted by permission.

Virginia Satir, *Peoplemaking*. Palo Alto, CA: Science Behavior Books, 1972, 27–29. Reprinted by permission.

New World Library is dedicated to publishing books and
cassettes that help improve the quality of our lives.

For a catalog of our fine books
and cassettes, contact:

New World Library
58 Paul Drive
San Rafael, CA 94903
Phone: (415) 472-2100
FAX: (415) 472-6131

Or call toll free:
(800) 227-3900
In California: (800) 632-2122